POLITICS AND ADMINISTRATIVE JUSTICE

Postliberalism, Street-Level
Bureaucracy and the Reawakening
of Democratic Citizenship

Nick O'Brien

BRISTOL
UNIVERSITY
PRESS

First published in Great Britain in 2025 by

Bristol University Press
University of Bristol
1–9 Old Park Hill
Bristol
BS2 8BB
UK
t: +44 (0)117 374 6645
e: bup-info@bristol.ac.uk

Details of international sales and distribution partners are available at bristoluniversitypress.co.uk

British Library Cataloguing in Publication Data
A catalogue record for this book is available from the British Library

ISBN 978-1-5292-3058-1 hardcover
ISBN 978-1-5292-3059-8 paperback
ISBN 978-1-5292-3060-4 ePub
ISBN 978-1-5292-3061-1 ePdf

Cover design: Blu inc
Front cover image: Alamy/Wirestock, Inc.

To Poornima and Izzy

Contents

About the Author

Nick O'Brien qualified as a solicitor in 1987 and has held senior positions at the offices of the Legal Services Ombudsman for England and Wales, the Disability Rights Commission and the UK Parliamentary Ombudsman and Health Service Ombudsman for England. He has been a part-time tribunal judge, specialist adviser to the House of Commons Public Administration Select Committee and an honorary research fellow at the School of Law and Social Justice, University of Liverpool. In 2019, he won the *Political Quarterly*'s Bernard Crick Prize. He is the co-author, with Mary Seneviratne, of *Ombudsmen at the Crossroads: The Legal Services Ombudsman, Dispute Resolution and Democratic Accountability* (Palgrave Macmillan, 2017), and, with Margaret Doyle, of *Reimagining Administrative Justice: Human Rights in Small Places* (Palgrave Macmillan, 2019).

Acknowledgements

I would like to thank the following for their valuable comments on earlier drafts: Margaret Doyle, Kevin Kearns, Richard Kirkham, Bob Niven and Poornima O'Brien.

1

Introduction

The world of everyday citizen grievance is remote from the concerns of high politics and public policy, an apparently unfortunate manifestation of a 'culture of complaint' marked by personal disaffection, self-interest and collective alienation. The work of those whose professional lives, as street-level bureaucrats, case reviewers, mediators, tribunal members and ombudsman ('ombud') staff, are consumed in responding to such grievances in turn appears a necessary but largely unrewarding enterprise. Hermetically sealed from mainstream political thought, the contemporary 'grievance culture', occasionally interrogated for 'lessons learned' and 'market surveillance' purposes, is largely relegated to the awkward margins of polite conversation. When it percolates into political consciousness, it is likely to be in the context of rarefied debate about the constitutional implications of judicial review or the tragic drama of set-piece public inquiry, far removed from the ordinary and the quotidian.

The everyday ways of responding more routinely to citizen grievance, what might be called 'administrative justice' (as opposed to 'administrative law'), are nevertheless a constantly moving target, subject to periodic adjustment and organizational tinkering. Law Commission reports, White Papers and select committee inquiries accumulate; processes for making official decisions and providing redress are constantly in flux. Yet despite national and regional variation, with notably more striking innovation in the devolved nations of the UK than in England, options for reform rarely escape the constraints of a legalistic form of consumerism. At best, citizen grievance assumes an instrumental purpose much like that of a disaffected focus group, to be managed more efficiently; at worst, it is perceived as largely irrelevant to democratic politics. Periodic change, halting and incremental, is technocratic and hygienic, the preferred recipe 'more of the same'. When the UK Administrative Justice and Tribunals Council was abolished in 2013, together with its ambition of holistic oversight, its demise was greeted with little more than a muffled murmur of political dissent.

This book offers an alternative perspective drawn from the ordinary culture of 'the street', not the extraordinary ambience of judicial review in the High Court or of public inquiry. It claims for citizen grievance a measure of value that, far from being solely instrumental, is inherent to its place at the interface between street and state. By displacing the perception that street-level bureaucracy is passive and incidental to policy and law-making, a matter of mere implementation, it in turn proposes that those agencies, charged with the task of responding to grievance, both within public authorities and especially beyond, have a function that is itself inherently political. That such a perception is not more widely shared can be attributed to the tenacious hold on the collective imagination of a form of legalism that saps political energy and builds around administrative justice a defensive wall that is impermeable to political comprehension. Left to its own devices, and to the scrutiny of a handful of specialists, administrative justice, unlike its civil justice and criminal justice counterparts, is, in England at least, and beyond the confines of judicial review and public inquiry, cut off from mainstream political debate and sustainable innovation.

That such a situation prevails is made more surprising by the association of legalism with a set of assumptions and ways of proceeding that, in an increasingly postliberal era, are under sustained pressure. The supremacy of command-and-control systems of public management, centralized supervision, enforceable rules and adversarialism has long been threatened by reflexive, communitarian and problem-solving alternatives that seek their credibility in an ethos which, while not disavowing the many achievements of political liberalism, nevertheless asserts a postliberal emancipation from its limitations. In a post-pandemic moment, that emancipatory quest has acquired new urgency, creating new opportunity. The reimagining of administrative justice is one such opportunity, and with it the prospect, in its renewed practice, of a reawakening of participatory democratic citizenship that is affirmative, humane and necessarily political (Doyle and O'Brien, 2020). Administrative justice is everyday justice, and its politics the politics of the everyday (Stears, 2021).

Since the early 1960s, British film director Ken Loach has chronicled with piercing insight the street-life of Britain and its complex relationship with the state, both local and national. While his cinematic journey may not have taken him literally to Wigan Pier, his descent into the underworld of poverty and disadvantage has had about it an Orwellian ambience, his subjects ranging from homelessness to industrial strife, mental distress to life on welfare benefits, and, more recently, to the gig economy and the refugee crisis. His has been 'art in the service of the people' (Leigh, 2002), yet it is an art that has also been alert to the relationships between citizens and public authorities, and to the inherently political quality of the everyday grievances they generate. In *Cathy Come Home* (Sandford, 1976), his classic

1966 TV film about homelessness on the streets of Britain, the besuited local authority housing officers interview Cathy across a desk with their backs to the camera, unrecognizable by the viewer. These anonymous, and faceless, representatives of the state evoke the apparent remoteness of bystanders to the tragedy of everyday life. It is an encounter between state and street that expresses social distance and conjures the spectre of mutual alienation. In his later commentary on the film, Loach made it clear that his presentation of local authority officers, caught between the competing demands of official policy and everyday human need, was not without sympathy. Far from being the "villains of the piece", they were instead simply "the people who had to administer the unworkable situation that existed" (Lacey, 2011: 79–80).

Fifty years later, in *I, Daniel Blake* (2016), Loach presented an equally nuanced picture of street-level bureaucrats in the north-east of England as they respond with varying degrees of civility to the competing pressures of administration in an era of neoliberalism and the New Public Management, which introduced to the public sector values of competition and consumerism more commonly associated with the private sector (O'Brien, 2018). For Daniel Blake, the beleaguered welfare benefit claimant, the contemporary tags of 'client', 'customer' and 'service user' elicit an experience of alienation as profound as that of 1960s homelessness. It is a sense of alienation that rejects 'victim' status, despite the indignity of the 'work capability assessment' and the sanctions that follow. Refusing the euphemistic and patronizing lexicon of contemporary managerialism, Blake asserts his claim to dignity in an older, more humane language: "My name is Daniel Blake, I am a man, not a dog. As such, I demand my rights. I demand you treat me with respect. I, Daniel Blake, am a citizen, nothing more, nothing less" (Laverty and Loach, 2016: 133).

The depiction of oppressive state bureaucracy has since Loach's 1966 film become an increasingly lurid backdrop to life on the streets of Britain, the 'hostile environment' created in 2012 by the Home Office for immigrants seen by many as the characteristic ambience of state bureaucracy in general, both local and national. In a neoliberal era, its perceived hostility has extended far beyond the plight of asylum seekers to those who encounter need, marginalization and misfortune in all their contemporary guises. In 2022, the National Theatre in London put on a play called *All of Us*, written by disabled actor and activist Francesca Martinez about the *Catch-22* obstacle course faced by disabled people in Personal Independent Payment assessments (Martinez, 2022). An anthology of horror stories about the consequences of Department for Work and Pensions and local authority budget cuts, the production drew upon the experience of the cast, many of whom were themselves disabled people. Appositely, the first-night audience included Ken Loach: as one reviewer observed, at its best the play resembles his 'classic TV revelation of homelessness, *Cathy Come Home*, as a piece of urgent dramatic journalism' (Lawson, 2022: 22).

Yet as with Loach's films, Martinez's evocation of disadvantage resists the easy polarities of victimhood and state oppression. The title of the play, albeit with some irony, evokes the idea so beloved of some political leaders that 'we are all in this together', even when it is obvious to most that some of us are a lot more 'in it' than others. Nevertheless, the recognition of shared human vulnerability is enough to show that no one is entirely safe. Individual officials, and even politicians, are themselves caught up in a game of chance that defies logic or easy explanation. As for Loach, so for Martinez, the common ground and potential source of salvation is that of shared citizenship, membership of a political community that holds out the prospect of meaning and dignity. It is during a public meeting that the play's disabled protagonists confront their local Tory MP, find their respective voices and express their justified grievance. Their manifesto is that of Daniel Blake, a reassertion of their status as citizens, nothing more, nothing less.

In an era that increasingly attracts the epithet 'postliberal', there is an urgent need to engage more generally with emerging political debates of this sort about the relationship between the citizen and the state, and with opportunities for reimagining that relationship. 'Liberalism' is a 'slippery term with many meanings' (Pabst, 2019: 5). Economic liberalism evokes laissez-faire and market capitalism, while social liberalism conveys the sense of cultural toleration. Political liberalism, with which this book is primarily concerned, has different connotations either side of the Atlantic: in North America, it denotes support for a moderately generous form of welfarism, while in Britain the connotation is notably more libertarian. For political theorists, political liberalism similarly takes various forms, that associated with philosophers John Rawls and Ronald Dworkin marked by a strain of egalitarianism that is largely absent from the more full-bloodedly libertarian variants favoured by others such as Robert Nozick and Friedrich Hayek. What they have in common is attachment to a form of 'liberal legalism' that prioritizes the 'philosophy of right' over the 'philosophy of the good'. Individual rights, negative liberty and individual identity are the keywords, freedom amounting to little more than the absence of unlawful constraint on individual choice. For liberal legalism, what matters is what is right, and what is right is what is just – and what is just is whatever the law requires, as adjudicated upon by court-type institutions (sometimes, but not always actual courts) that meet variously prescribed forms and procedures. Such formalism and proceduralism pay scant attention to substantive justice and democratic equality, since to dwell in that way on 'ends' rather than 'means' would run the risk of indulging a teleological ambition that sits uneasily with liberal disinterestedness about the content of the good life.

The political liberalism with which this book is concerned, and to which postliberalism might be described as 'post', is to that extent the contemporary form of liberalism, associated especially with Rawls and his epochal *A Theory of Justice* (1971), for which nothing much is left to political decision: 'The basic liberties and the distribution of social goods are matters of justice, and in political liberalism what justice demands is a matter not for political decision but for legal adjudication', the irony being that political liberalism turns out to be not very political at all and instead a 'species of anti-political legalism' (Gray, 2000: 16).

A form of postliberalism that rejects both populist and authoritarian alternatives to contemporary liberalism is one that instead, like Loach's films and Martinez's play, invites the re-awakening of democratic citizenship in a form that is decidedly participatory. If the keywords for contemporary liberalism are individual rights, negative liberty and individual identity, for the postliberal alternative they are the common good, positive liberty and inclusive community enabled not just by the centralized liberal state but by the dispersed authority of civic association.

Postliberalism in this sense should not be confused with a simple re-hash of the communitarian ideas of the 1980s and 1990s, still less with merely Third Way or Big Society aspirations. Powerful though communitarian critiques of contemporary liberalism were, their idealization of homogeneous community at times turned to an admiration for 'common life-forms' that smacked of 'polis-nostalgia' and uneasiness with pluralist modernity. Moreover, it was admiration that failed for the most part to extend to associations that were not of an entirely local kind, and so excluded from its gaze other forms of association that depended on more than local bonds of affectionate proximity.

Postliberalism of the type invoked here seeks to preserve the best of both communitarianism and liberalism, valuing the shared determination of meanings and values, while insisting that this sharing will not result in a homogeneous society but in exactly the plurality that liberalism so admires. Such a conjuring trick is made possible by what cultural critic Terry Eagleton, in a somewhat different context, has called 'the crucial ambiguity' of the term 'common culture', which can mean both 'commonly shared' and 'commonly made' (Eagleton, 1967, 1994). As Eagleton suggests, it would be a mistake to think that the latter implies the former; on the contrary, 'the truth is that if everyone is able to participate fully in the definition of that culture, then it is likely to end up a good deal more heterogeneous than it is if its values are formulated by an elite' (Eagleton, 1994: 300). A measure of shared value there will surely be on account of its 'collective democratic fashioning', but within that common framework there will be 'ceaseless conflict and negotiation between the interests which those structures have enabled to be voiced' (Eagleton, 1994: 300). Since versions of the good life do not come with 'metaphysical seals of approval' baked in, there is no alternative but 'to argue the toss over them', and that activity of arguing the toss is known as the exercise of reason (Eagleton, 1994: 303). The rule of reason rather than the rule of law as the rule of rights or the rule of rules has priority.

Acknowledging a central function of politics as precisely the reasoned conciliation of estranged interests in pursuit of the common good and recognizing the importance of public administration itself as a democratic and deliberative forum, the chapters that follow more specifically ask what part the response to citizen grievance by administrative justice institutions, especially tribunals, civic mediators and ombuds, might play in the realization of that conciliatory project. In both *I, Daniel Blake* and *All of Us*, the prospect of a 'tribunal' as potential source of resolution is dangled before the audience but in neither case quite realized. The audience is instead left uncertain whether deliverance would in fact have been achieved if only those aggrieved had been afforded their 'day in court'. In responding to citizen grievance, such institutions, although not precisely 'courts', are themselves unavoidably implicated in an activity that is integral to the maintenance of democratic culture in everyday life and to the democratic task of 'going on together' (Ober, 2005). How they do so carries political and social weight.

Public administration is central to the way citizens discover and perceive their relationship with the state. Administrative justice, the business of 'doing justice' by responding to citizen grievance about public administration, in turn warrants political recognition not just as an aspect of public law but as a means of realizing a more participatory form of democratic citizenship. In recent years, health and social care maladministration, the provision of mental health services, public housing, welfare benefits and immigration policy-implementation have captured the headlines in Britain. Elsewhere, and more dramatically, the Arab Spring has been interpreted as an event sparked by the indignities inflicted by the state at street-level, and by its inability to engage humanely, and in the spirit of democratic values, with its citizens (Ben Jelloun, 2016). Yet, often despite the intentions of their originators, the means for addressing such concerns have remained in thrall to a particular brand of legalism that stifles the possibility of transformational intervention. By evoking a form of postliberalism in which the classical liberal emphasis on individual rights and their legal enforcement is counterbalanced by alternative emphases, the book aims to promote the positive potential of administrative justice as an incipiently postliberal, democratic and egalitarian set of aspirations and practices.

The narrative that unfolds seeks not to undermine the emancipatory gains of liberalism but to draw upon the resources available to postliberal thinking from intellectual traditions within mainstream liberalism that have become marginalized. Four such strands capture the need for re-emphasis: philosophical Idealism, political pluralism, civic humanism, and pragmatism. These marginalized strands of thought serve to reassert counterbalancing emphases to the legalistic form of contemporary liberalism: the positive value of the ethical state working in partnership with civil society as an instrument of the common good (philosophical Idealism); the value of intermediate association and dispersed, polycentric governance (political pluralism); the primacy of human character, dignity and solidaristic citizenship as a framework for developmental, participatory and humane practice (civic humanism); and an experiential and problem-solving approach to democratic governance (pragmatism). The primary aim of the book will be to suggest that renewed possibilities for administrative justice institutions coalesce with these emergent postliberal themes, and so serve as a portal to a renewed politics of participatory democratic citizenship. Administrative justice is ordinary and its political context that of everyday democracy.

To bring a distinctive and concrete perspective to bear on these considerations, the book will take inspiration from what has been described as the 'new paradigm' of disability human rights, especially as articulated in the UN Convention on the Rights of Persons with Disabilities. It will be argued, by way of specific reference to response to grievances about the mental health system and the special educational needs and disability (SEND) system, that this new paradigm foreshadows much that is necessary for the postliberal alternative and represents an especially valuable resource for making that alternative real.

The notable 'paradigm shift' heralded by the advent of disability as a central component of contemporary understandings of equality and human rights is part of a broader revival of humanistic values shaped by the emerging discourse of 'disability'. The broad philosophical implications have sparked the interest of thinkers as varied as Alasdair MacIntyre, Julia Kristeva and Martha Nussbaum. MacIntyre, author of *After Virtue* (1981), later acknowledged that in that pioneering work of virtue ethics he had entirely overlooked the question of 'what makes attention to human vulnerability and disability important for moral philosophers?' (MacIntyre, 1999). In later work, he sought to address that omission by explicitly recognizing that it is through encounter with disability that it becomes possible to gain unrivalled insight into human interdependency (MacIntyre, 1999: 136).

Kristeva, in her reflections on hatred and forgiveness translated from the French in 2010, similarly found privileged access to the experience of exclusion from recognizing the pervasiveness of physical and mental impairment, and the need to transform visceral fear and hatred into 'attention, patience and solidarity capable of refining my being in the world' (Kristeva, 2010: 266).

More expansively, Nussbaum, in expounding the 'human development approach' to capability articulated over many years in collaboration with Nobel Prize-winning economist and philosopher Amartya Sen, has drawn sustained attention to the challenging implications of disability for the entire structure of dominant notions of 'justice as fairness' and for the contractarian theory on which it stands (Nussbaum, 2006, 2011). As she observes of such theory, 'the basic structure of society is mapped out' without including people with physical and mental impairment, who are overlooked entirely as potential parties to the social contract; yet realism demands recognition that 'we all have many impairments' and periods more or less prolonged of 'unusual and asymmetrical dependency' (Nussbaum, 2004: 312). If we are to create social conditions of self-respect for all, we must devise ways of recognizing and supporting the full humanity and individuality of disabled people. The conception of the citizen as an 'independent bargainer' must be replaced by a 'more complex image of a being both capable and needy, who moves from helplessness to "mutual interdependence", and, unfortunately, often back to helplessness again' (Nussbaum, 2004: 312–13). The challenge then for contemporary liberalism, and for the strains of legalism within its dominant imaginary, becomes the achievement of a form that does not, in its unrealistic abstractions, entail 'hiding from humanity' (Nussbaum, 2004).

Francis Fukuyama is most frequently associated with the 'end of history' version of liberalism that in a neoliberal guise has sought especially since 1989 to assume mastery of the social, political and economic domains. In his most recent work, Fukuyama has nevertheless drawn attention to liberalism's discontents and to the way in which it has been distorted by pushing to extremes some of its dearest values, without due recognition of the need for limits (Fukuyama, 2022). As Fukuyama suggests, if a measure of economic freedom is good, it does not follow that the removal of all economic constraints by neoliberalism will make it even better; nor should respect for personal autonomy as the source of individual fulfilment entail that unlimited freedom and incessant disruption of constraint invariably make for ever more personal flourishing. For Fukuyama, a key feature of a reinvigorated liberalism should be its adoption of the ancient Greek exhortation *meden agan* ('nothing in excess'), notwithstanding the contemporary suspicion of the cool tone of compromise such an exhortation can sometimes be taken to evoke (Fukuyama, 2022: 154).

In a similar spirit, the invocation of postliberalism should not be taken to denote a form of anti-liberalism or retreat into a type of polis-nostalgia that associates the achievement of the common good with the rigorous exercise of moral authority, 'thick' cultural bonds and exclusive forms of social homogeneity. Instead, postliberalism invites a recalibration of liberalism's priorities and emphases. In the case of administrative justice, that is a recalibration that questions the centrality of liberal legalism as its defining mentality or 'social imaginary'.

The COVID-19 pandemic which gripped the world in early 2020 represents a point of rupture and an opportunity for that exercise in recalibration. Such recalibration offers the prospect of a new equilibrium, a different weighing of priorities. However much there is a desire to return to 'normality' and to the way things were, as with other similar ruptures such a return is both unrealistic and unwise: all is changed, changed utterly. The pandemic is a portal, a gateway to something new. As novelist and social activist Arundhati Roy has observed: 'We can choose to walk through it, dragging the carcasses of our prejudice and hatred, our avarice, our data banks and dead ideas, our dead rivers and smoky skies behind us. Or we can walk through lightly, with little luggage, ready to imagine another world' (Roy, 2020: 214).

The plan of the book

The chapters that follow will seek to travel lightly, in the sense implied by Roy. Chapter 2 situates the discussion in the context of bureaucracy as a problem in relationships between citizens and state. It sets the scene by proposing that, notwithstanding technological change, the everyday relationships between street-level bureaucrats and citizens remain the critical interface of the democratic state, and that public authorities are as a result the linchpins of democratic practice. Both sides of that relationship are therefore deserving of careful nurture, especially when the relationship is in danger of breaking down, as in the case of citizen complaint. It is in the orchestration of those relationships that administrative justice institutions such as tribunals, ombuds and civic mediators have a crucial, broadly political, role to play and the opportunity to achieve an accountability dividend that adds democratic value. Three different modes of legality – repressive, autonomous and responsive – are introduced as a framework for identifying alternative approaches to accountability.

Chapter 3 considers the way in which liberal legalism has limited the scope of administrative justice institutions in responding innovatively to citizen grievance. It proposes that liberal legalism constitutes more than a set of techniques and is instead an outlook or mentality that can best be described, in the terminology of philosopher Charles Taylor, as an entire 'social imaginary'. It exposes the key characteristics and expressions of that social imaginary as an aspect of autonomous legality, linking it to rights-based adversarialism, the common law mind and modern constitutionalism. It concludes with cultural representations of the judge as a concrete image of repressive and autonomous legalities, respectively.

Chapter 4 looks to postliberalism as a means of salvation from liberal legalism. It emphasizes the value of the common good against the priority of individual rights, while also warning against the seductions of a form of common good constitutionalism that threatens to undermine democratic pluralism. To counter the centrality of legalism for contemporary liberalism, it aims to reinstate aspects of liberal thought that have become recessive: philosophical Idealism, political pluralism, civic humanism and political pragmatism. In this way, it seeks to emphasize the importance for postliberalism of the positive and ethical state, of the individual as socially embedded in civil society, of virtuous disposition, dignity and character, and of problem-solving, both particular and general, as the affirmative purpose of response to grievance. It concludes with cultural representation of the responsive justice that resides in the common good as an answer to that of the repressive or autonomous judge.

Chapter 5 glances back to the interwar years for illustration from the public administration literature in Britain of debates about the response to grievance that were wary of liberal legalism and held out the prospect of a tribunal system that was very different from the courts. It similarly recounts the postwar ambitions for an entirely innovative, informal and democratic means of shaping the relationship between citizen and state, based on the Scandinavian institution of the 'ombudsman'. It aims to show how in the case of both tribunals and ombuds, those extra-judicial ambitions foundered on liberal legalism, so that tribunals became subject to a gradual process of judicialization and the public ombuds to containment as essentially constitutional and legal offices.

Chapter 6 serves as a hinge that opens the door to the second half of the book. It argues that the consolidation of disability human rights since the 1990s offers a new impetus for reviving those incipiently postliberal aspirations for response to citizen grievance. It draws on the development of disability rights in Britain, the practical strategy of the Disability Rights Commission between 2000 and 2007, and the emergence of the UN Convention on the Rights of Persons with Disabilities as turning points in the reconstruction of a postliberal and responsive legality that accentuates the role of the ethical state, the importance of partnership between citizens and state, the dignity of the human person and the pragmatic ambition of purposive problem-solving when the citizen–state relationship is in danger of breaking down.

Chapter 7 examines how far the priorities emerging from disability human rights have been realized in the way in which grievances are handled in the mental health and SEND systems in England. It considers the historical trajectory of developments in both contexts and identifies the key challenges in each as relating to the positive function of the state and to the active participation of both street-level bureaucrats and citizens. It draws upon comparative illustration to suggest that social advocacy in case-conferencing tribunals, positive social rights intervention by ombuds and forms of civic 'mediation' that are deliberative and problem-solving rather than primarily adjudicatory are in continuing tension with legalistic constraints that threaten to inhibit responsive legality and postliberal emphases.

Chapter 8 turns from the specific context of disability human rights to the broader terrain of public administration and street-level bureaucracy in other contexts. It proposes three key focal points for the construction of postliberal administrative justice: the citizen-agency of street-level bureaucrats, alongside the democratic culture of public authorities; the active participation of aggrieved citizens in finding solutions to the problems revealed by their grievances; and the bridging capacity of administrative justice institutions in the development of social advocacy, 'participatory readiness' and purposive intervention. From that foundation, it builds a framework for a postliberal accountability strategy that emphasizes the practical function of public authorities as the vehicles of democratic agency, of civic association as a source of social advocacy, of the individual as a democratic and participative citizen, and of administrative justice institutions as integrated, dispersed, problem-solving and bridging institutions. It concludes by way of illustration with the practical application of such emphases to the specific social problem of the exclusion of pupils from school.

Finally, Chapter 9 by way of conclusion offers an overview of the main themes. It provides a postliberal interpretation of the democratic quality of public authorities and street-level bureaucracy; it rehearses the main characteristics of a postliberalism that is marked by responsive legality in the way it orchestrates the response to citizen grievance; and it suggests that for postliberalism the justice inherent in public administration is the everyday justice of the common good and to that extent something more than 'administrative justice' as conventionally conceived, with all the inherent political possibility that such enlargement entails. In a postliberal world, administrative justice is unavoidably complicit with, and best characterized as, a form of 'post-legalism'.

2

Street-Level Bureaucracy and the Response to Citizen Grievance

The everyday quality of interactions between citizen and state, and the grievances they generate, should not be taken to denote a relationship that is simple and easily construed as one of inherent oppression. Street-level bureaucracy is a site of complexity, governed by its own fragile ecosystem. Individual grievance is similarly complex and socially embedded, situated in a social context that requires the cultivation of an 'art of complaining' that is a function of civic maturity. For those agencies charged with the task of responding to citizen grievance, constructive intervention that adds value and achieves an accountability dividend must be attuned to the complex relationships it encounters at street-level. Retreat behind a legal framework that too readily finds in law an autonomous instrument of control, insulated from complex and changing social reality, is an evasion that diminishes the possibility of transformational intervention in the name of administrative justice.

Bureaucracy and citizenship

'A problem in relationships'

While the COVID-19 pandemic has turned the spotlight on 'key workers' and their undervalued social contribution, the wave of support for supermarket cashiers and delivery drivers has scarcely extended to those whose daily tasks are seen as tainted by state bureaucracy. The heroism attributed to those on the frontline of service delivery has remained largely inaccessible to those whose encounters with the public take place across a desk, office counter or, more often, mobile phone-call or computer video-link. Despite the advance of modern technology, the 'desk' remains a significant metaphor in the context of encounters between street and state, the site, in a small place, of their separation and of their different roles, identities and levels of power: in short, 'the desk is a physical place where state–citizen encounters occur, but it is also a symbol of state authority' (Dubois, 2016; Maynard-Moody, 2016: ix). Even in the contemporary world of virtual and digital bureaucracy, the notion of street-level encounter between frontline workers and individual citizens remains valid. In their contact with citizens as consumers and clients, pupils and parents, patients, tenants and vehicle drivers, street-level bureaucrats continue to function as the bearers of inherent discretion, policy co-producers and exponents of a distinctive occupational craft (Hupe et al, 2016: 16).

Yet the prevailing sense of contradiction experienced by key workers and the sub-set of that group that constitutes street-level bureaucracy is in crucial respects of similar origin. For key workers and street-level bureaucrats, the structure of their work leaves them exposed to the crosscurrents of organizational policy as it plays out in the real world, far away from the drawing-board and lecture hall. Invariably, frontline workers find themselves at the bottom of the organizational hierarchy, required to interact directly with the public, and, although having limited decision-making power, nevertheless able to exercise their responsibilities with a meaningful margin of discretion, even if extended only grudgingly. It is the residually discretionary character of their agency that freights their work with moral jeopardy. In the tangle of their relationships – with the public, with colleagues, with managers, with 'the system' – street-level bureaucrats must learn to navigate the uncertain waters that lie between policy and implementation, rules and practice, law in the books and law in action.

Even before the pandemic, the 'dismemberment' of the state had taken a heavy toll on the ethos of public service in Britain (Toynbee and Walker, 2017). Conversations with NHS staff, and with central and local government officials, led Polly Toynbee and David Walker to conclude that if the state is to be reconfigured, many of those working on its behalf must submit to a process of 'metamorphosis', in which they abandon their contemporary fatalism and, just as importantly, shed themselves of 'New Public Management precepts'. In some instances, they will even have to discard the attire of their political bosses and the mantle of public service transformer that comes with enthusiasm for streamlining and contracting out (Toynbee and Walker, 2017: 158). As Sir David Nicholson, former CEO of the NHS, remarked to a select committee hearing on public-sector complaints in 2014, it is time to move on from the language of targets and permanent change, of "aiming higher", "driving forward" and "pace setting" (Public Administration Select Committee, 2014: 43).

Ever since the ground-breaking investigations of street-level bureaucracy and 'bureaucratic justice' by American scholars Michael Lipsky and Jerry Mashaw in the 1980s, there has been heightened awareness of the tension inherent in the role of frontline public agents. For Lipsky, the challenge was to create a structure of work that would be more likely to produce effective 'service-providers', better attuned to the needs of the public but also capable of reducing the dissonance between their own expectations and the outcomes achievable (Lipsky, 1980). Mashaw characterized the different ways of describing possible interactions between citizen and state according to one of three models: bureaucratic rationality, professional treatment, and moral judgement (Mashaw, 1983). More recent socio-legal analyses have expanded the frames of reference to include values explicitly associated with consumerism and managerialism, or that reflect, through the application of 'grid and group' theory, different underlying cultural biases of the sort articulated by social anthropologist Mary Douglas (Adler, 2003, 2006; Halliday and Scott, 2010; Kirkham, 2022). Drawing on these analyses, some have emphasized the precarious 'legal consciousness' of public agents (Hertogh, 2018); others have directed attention beyond a focus on the quality of individual decision-making by considering demands not only for 'putting it right' but for 'getting it right' in the first place and for 'setting right' administrative justice in a broader policy and constitutional environment (Buck et al, 2011); still others draw attention to the need to transcend bureaucratic, legal or individual justice altogether, replacing it with explicit concern for 'therapeutic justice' or for 'social justice' as the overriding objective in responding to citizen grievance and as part of the 'new administrative law' (Nason, 2016, 2019; Nason et al, 2020; Creutzfeldt et al, 2021; Gulland, 2022; Stuhmcke, 2022; Williams et al, 2022). Yet for the most part, a Weberian shadow still falls across the 'problem of bureaucracy': rules, compliance and control are the trinity of factors informing questions that take conformity and deviance as their starting point.

Writing in 1949, W. H. Morris Jones, then a lecturer in political science at the London School of Economics, remarked of the problem of bureaucracy that '[i]n essence, it is a problem in relationships', and any solution is 'almost certain to call for a positive contribution of citizen participation in some form or other' (Morris Jones, 1949: 28–9). Rejecting the supposition that public authorities are 'mere devices or pieces of dead machinery', Morris Jones warned that '[w]e must see that to all institutions there adhere attitudes and loyalties which help to make the spirit which inform their working, and also that institutions are part of a more general context of national life from which they can only with danger be dissociated'; the problem of bureaucracy is not, he suggests, one 'that admits of solution in purely organisational terms' (Morris Jones, 1949: 29).

The 'ethnographic turn'

The current need for retreat from technocratic, managerial or organizational solutions towards a more nuanced concern with 'the problem in relationships' is made more apparent by the 'ethnographic turn' in political theory and in recent studies of public agencies (Brodkin, 2017; Longo and Zacka, 2019). The ethnographic turn aims more tenaciously to get under the skin of street-level bureaucrats and the public agencies in which they work and thereby expose in a distinctive way the inner workings of the state. The primary focus is not exclusively on 'how institutions think' (Douglas, 1987) but as much on how they imagine and feel, on how they construct concrete practices and 'cultures' that shape relationships formed in response to those imaginings and feelings. Such ethnographic approaches aim to build a vision of the state from the bottom up in a manner that is inductive and micropolitical. According to such an approach, the state is quite simply what its agents do 'under the multiple influences of the policies they implement, the habits they develop, the initiatives they take, and the responses they get from their publics' (Fassin, 2015: ix). It is in the interstices of such practices that the tensions and contradictions of public agency are made manifest. The implications of such an ethnographic approach are notable, not just for interpreting the behaviour of street-level bureaucrats, but for assessing the importance of such behaviour in a democratic context. Far from street-level bureaucrats being the passive implementers of previously determined law and policy, they become under the searchlight of ethnographic investigation the active makers of law and policy in action.

In a series of 'stories from the frontlines of public services' in the US, the authors of a study published in 2003 draw a distinction between what they describe as a 'state-agent narrative' and a 'citizen-agent narrative'. According to the former narrative, the democratic state is built on law and predictable procedures, with a firm boundary separating the making of law and policy from their bureaucratic implementation. Public administration emerges in turn as a means of confining and channelling the exercise of discretion, which is at best viewed as an undesirable but unavoidable form of deviance. According to the latter narrative, however, social relationships, rather than formal duties and responsibilities as defined by law and policy, provide the real context in which street-level bureaucrats operate: 'In their narratives, street-level workers also define their work and to a large extent themselves in terms of their relationships more than rules'; in this way, their decisions and actions are guided 'as much by meaning as by function' (Maynard-Moody and Musheno, 2003: 20).

The assembled stories reinforce the view that in the real world of street-level bureaucracy it is the citizen-agent narrative which prevails. According to that narrative, street-level bureaucrats emerge as 'empowered citizen agents' who have it in their gift to legitimate the state and 'convey the status of citizenship' in the way they allocate resources, provide access to welfare programmes and impose sanctions. The passivity derived from the orthodox state-agent narrative is on this account transfigured into active agency, street-level bureaucracy itself the forum in which citizens gain privileged access to the texture of the state: 'More than demonstrating that they are enforcers or implementers of law, street-level workers' narratives indicate that they are citizen-agents who help produce and maintain society's normative, as much as legal, order' (Maynard-Moody and Musheno, 2003: 24).

Ethnographic work among French street-level bureaucrats in the 1990s similarly disclosed the way in which those on the bottom rungs of the hierarchy in two family-benefit field-offices made full use of their opportunities to exercise social agency alongside their official role as agents of the state. This dichotomy led the study's author, Vincent Dubois, to refer to the 'two bodies' of street-level bureaucrats: embodiments of the state, yet also of civil society in their responsiveness to complex need as manifest on 'the street'. In exercising discretion, welfare workers 'make arrangements' and take 'small liberties', so that they can apply the rules purposively. They do not so much 'implement' public policy as attend to its 'materialization', making real the abstractions conceived in the boardroom (Dubois, 2016).

Such perceptions are reinforced by Bernardo Zacka, whose ethnographic reflections based on eight months of participant-observation in a government welfare programme in the US aim to bring political theory and moral philosophy into conversation with psychology, sociology and anthropology (Zacka, 2017). For Zacka, 'the street' is not a 'passive target or receptacle for the law' but instead 'contributes to shaping what the law means', representing the moment when universal norms encounter the particular and thereby acquire practical meaning (Zacka, 2017: 248). Moreover, the ways in which such street-level encounters occur are critical to the successful working of the democratic state. The operation of street-level bureaucracy is a mirror, in which democratic citizens get a glimpse of themselves, a mirror that is often more truthful than abstract law and policy, precisely 'because it involves deeds rather than words' (Zacka, 2017: 253). It is critical for public trust that the moral personality of street-level bureaucracy is one in which democratic citizens can indeed recognize themselves without averting their gaze in shame from shocking distortion of their collective self-image. The claims made for the importance of street-level bureaucracy transcend the instrumental and technocratic prerogatives of service-delivery, and of rules, compliance and control. They are claims instead that go to the heart of the democratic state and how it perceives itself. They go to the heart also of democratic citizenship, to the exercise of power and discretion on the one hand, and of effective citizen-participation on the other.

Public authorities: redefining the 'basic structure'

The 'linchpins' of democratic practice

Mashaw's ground-breaking book, *Bureaucratic Justice* (1983), is celebrated by socio-legal students for its enduringly influential models of administrative justice. Yet he concludes by musing more discursively on the perplexing absence in the public imagination of a positive symbol of bureaucracy. Whereas the judiciary enjoys the majesty of the Supreme Court and the legislature the 'democracy-reaffirming ritual of elections', the executive lacks comparable symbolism, its fleeting identification with presidential-style charismatic leadership ultimately misleading and disillusioning. As Mashaw puts it: 'Our constitutional myth is that liberal democracy requires political leadership tied to electoral politics, with individual rights guaranteed by judicially administered law. Bureaucratic wielding of power is deviant: there is no constitutional office upon which it can be modelled' (Mashaw, 1983: 225).

Attempts to intervene in the task of holding to account street-level bureaucrats are confined because of this constitutional myth to the binary options either of forcing administrators into judicial moulds or of ensuring their compliance ever more rigorously with the perceived democratic will as expressed in prescriptive legislation. It is the law either as legislation or litigation which ensnares the imagination, captivating it with its promise of order, control and predictability. The result is a gap, as Mashaw observes, that cannot be filled merely by a change in the style of litigation.

The ethnographic turn in the investigation of the administrative state deepens the sense of perplexity identified by Mashaw, complicating the perception of public administration, its character, purpose and potential, and complicating too the question of how response to citizen grievance might be made more constructive. In the contemporary public imagination, bureaucracy is perceived negatively, as a source of obstruction, red tape and inefficiency, and as a self-serving machine that saps the energy of popular democracy. That Weberian perception arises from a liberal model of democracy that sees street-level bureaucrats and the public agencies they inhabit as the culmination of a chain of representation that is linked to street-level through prior stages of election and debate in legislative assemblies. Ethnographic enquiry offers a different perspective according to which the democratic business of going on together starts on the street with concrete problems encountered by citizens and with collaborative efforts to find solutions. Public agencies are the democratic forum for that exercise in problem-solving, not as an alternative to representative democracy but as a complement to it. As such, they become the 'linchpins' of democratic practice, linking 'the delegated authority that flows from people to legislatures to public agencies with the problem-solving authority that emerges from their bottom-up facilitation of collaborative problem-solving' (Ansell, 2011: 192). If they are to discharge that function effectively, they must earn trust and discretion by demonstrating their competence 'at creatively aligning the public values expressed through representative democracy with public values expressed through collaborative problem-solving' (Ansell, 2011: 192). When public agencies fail to meet that expectation of competence, they incite the expression of citizen grievance. How administrative justice institutions respond to those grievances carries democratic weight. As the Weberian shadow recedes from that response, so there is room for illumination beyond the legalistic nooks and crannies of rules, compliance and control, and beyond the legalistic devices of litigation and adjudication as conventionally constructed.

Beyond the 'shadow of justice'

To make such a claim is more fundamentally to partake in a reappraisal of one of the essential building blocks of a form of liberal legalism that owes much of its power to the work of American liberal analytical philosopher John Rawls, as expounded in his *A Theory of Justice* (1971). That essential building block is what Rawls refers to as 'the basic structure', which can be taken to comprise the ground rules of a society, both 'the rules of the game' and the social institutions that make up the starting point for players of the game, the 'practice to contain all practices' (Forrester, 2019: 32–4). In her exposition of the intellectual context that embeds Rawls' analysis, Katrina Forrester has suggested that Rawls proposed a 'minimalist view of the state'. That minimalism was in turn a reflection of the 'constitutionalist anxiety about expansionary administrative and executive power, which had trained the institutional imagination of American postwar political scientists in a different direction from their European counterparts, with their long tradition of state theory' (Forrester, 2019: 32). According to such a perception, 'the basic structure was a practice to be regulated, justified, and evaluated as a whole. The depoliticizing assumptions of anti-interventionist pluralism were baked in' (Forrester, 2019: 33). As a result, the idea of the state as a 'site of administrative conflict and as a distinctive institutional agent' was 'attenuated' in Rawls' vision rather than conceived as a site of the 'quasi-autonomous realm of agency, power, and interests' (Forrester, 2019: 33). Insofar as Rawlsian theory extended its gaze to the functioning of institutions, its focus was 'more on the juridical and legislative institutions than the executive or bureaucracy he wanted to constrain' (Forrester, 2019: 33).

It is not therefore merely the recession of the Weberian shadow but, incipiently through the advance of postliberalism, of what Forrester calls the Rawlsian 'shadow of justice' that space is yielded for a mentality that is not in thrall to legalism but that offers a more positive construction of the state and administration. The ethnographic turn in political theory is one of the pressure-points that re-accentuates previously recessive themes such as the workplace (Cruddas, 2021), the 'defence of politics' (Crick, 1962) and 'the return of the political' (Mouffe, 1993). It invites revision of the 'basic structure' itself and its characterization of the state and administration as both passive and as something nevertheless consistently to be contained. Ethnographic work, such as that on which Zacka and others draw, should be seen therefore as part of that broader challenge to the coherence of the basic structure that frames contemporary liberalism. Dissatisfied with the abstractions of Rawlsian theory, that broader challenge seeks instead to probe more deeply, and concretely, the nature of the state and its administration in a postliberal era when the relationship between citizen and state is being reconfigured.

The accountability dividend

'A site of institutional phronesis'

In the postwar task of containing the ambitions of the interventionist state, its administration and the street-level bureaucrats who staff it, three primary modes of accountability have been dominant. The 'command-and-control' model of regulation largely accepted the Weberian diagnosis of modernity and its hierarchical, impersonal character. At the heart of Weber's diagnosis was a system based on legal rationality that draws a sharp distinction between politics and public administration, that presumes and even reinforces a hierarchical structure of control, and that seeks to exercise that control through a system of rules. At a more fundamental level, such an approach privileges a conception of the rule of law as the rule of rules, the wishes of the electorate in a representative democracy being translated into concrete action through impersonal implementation by street-level bureaucrats (Ansell, 2011: 131–2). Although originally associated with US-style industrial management in the context of Henry Ford's system of mass production, command-and-control management had by the postwar period established itself as a powerful model of accountability, with easy application to the hierarchical structures of public agencies in emerging welfare states, such as Britain, and widespread acceptance as the 'classic' form of public regulation (Morgan and Yeung, 2007: 80–5).

In response to this postwar command-and-control approach, 'market-oriented utilitarians' sought to replace, or at least supplement, rules with incentives as a means of ensuring that public agents conformed to the wishes of their principals, and in turn effectively implemented the wishes of the electorate. Such an approach found expression most vividly in the New Public Management that took especially tenacious hold in liberal democracies during the 1980s, with the importation into public agencies of methods and styles of management from private business, street-level bureaucrats becoming accountable for results and 'outcomes' rather than merely formal compliance with 'the rules'.

A third variant of postwar regulation can be found in a contemporary approach that privileges 'transparency' and 'openness' as a strategy for ensuring compliance by public agencies. According to such an approach, citizens will still not enjoy direct participation in public decision-making processes but can nevertheless exercise a measure of scrutiny and vigilance, and so exert a check on negative behaviour. Importantly, what counts as 'negative behaviour' will be prescribed by 'constitutions' comprising codes of conduct, statements of principle and charters of standards, against which public agencies may be measured and by reference to which individual complaints may be launched, with the somewhat remote prospect of future 'learning' for errant organizations. Under such a regime, complaints are seen as 'gifts' that simply keep on giving. As a report of the House of Commons Select Committee on Public Administration illustrated in 2014, the abiding exhortation in that case becomes one of 'More Complaints, Please!' (Public Administration Select Committee, 2014).

All three models have in common a quest for certainty and a celebration of external control as both possible and desirable. The ethnographic turn casts doubt, however, on the validity of each of these three competing models, revealing them to be sources of disruption to the moral equilibrium that should otherwise prevail on the bureaucratic streets of a modern democracy: street-level alienation from codified standards is at least as likely as sustained commitment; the desire to emulate the private sector comes at a significant price, prioritizing efficiency over other democratic values; the reliance on rules and hierarchical control fails to take account of the complex and contradictory environment in which street-level bureaucrats construct identity and meaning.

By contrast to the three standard models, an alternative that draws upon ethnographic insight will recognize that street-level bureaucrats operate within a 'fragile moral ecosystem', for which the maintenance of democratic pluralism represents a 'delicate equilibrium' between competing values. It is of the essence of democratic practice that such balances are maintained as a means of reflecting the pluralistic values of a modern democratic polity. Street-level bureaucracy then becomes a 'site of institutionalized phronesis [practical wisdom], one where universal norms encounter particular cases and acquire practical meaning'; the process is not simply that of applying the law or implementing policy, but rather of its 'concretization' or 'materialization' in one of several available possibilities resulting from its contact with a particular situation (Zacka, 2017: 248). In that case, the challenge of effective accountability is not to replace discretion with formal structures, whether of rules, incentive or principle, but rather to 'orchestrate the environment in which individual agents develop self-understanding and exercise discretion'; such orchestration also entails acceptance of the autonomy of public agency as its cornerstone and of citizen participation as its mode of operation (Zacka, 2017: 246). It is in enabling such orchestration that the accountability dividend is cashed.

The art of complaining

Citizen participation in realizing the accountability dividend in turn entails cultivation of the art of complaining. For the most part, the practice of complaining has acquired a bad name in contemporary culture, its perceived prevalence identified as part of an unattractive 'culture of complaint' (Hughes, 1993). As philosopher Julian Baggini has observed, people tend to complain about 'the wrong things for the wrong reasons', with the result that 'complaining has been debased' (Baggini, 2008: 5). Yet complaining has a 'noble history' in whose chapters can be found the names of some of the most celebrated social reformers, from Emmeline Pankhurst to Martin Luther King and Nelson Mandela. On Baggini's analysis, the real culprit is a form of legalism, which encourages attempts to deal with misfortune by seeking legal redress: 'the overturning of morality by law is the recurrent pattern of grievance culture' (Baggini, 2008: 104). At a deeper philosophical level, this tendency towards legalism represents the triumph of Kantian notions of duty, obligation and the philosophy of right, and of utilitarian aspirations towards the maximizing of pleasure or happiness, at the expense of a richer ethical discourse that in the tradition of Aristotle focuses on the cultivation of virtuous dispositions and the philosophy of the good. One of the features of this advancing legalism is its promotion of the zero-sum game, in which complex ethical issues are reduced to binary, 'win or lose' options, and the belief that being in the right can brook no compromise: 'There is thus an objectivity to legal complaints which brokers no dispute, in contrast to moral complaints which always have to be argued for and can never be adjudicated with any finality' (Baggini, 2008: 108).

Objections to the 'grievance culture' have typically surfaced from those who see it as a function of the 'nanny state' and, with more than a whiff of nostalgia, a certain style of modern moral disintegration. Yet as Baggini points out, the chief source of such a culture is not state paternalism but the 'privatization of responsibility', the 'unfettered pursuit by individuals of their own personal interests' within the framework of the law, its 'legalistic discourse' promoting the value of 'accountability' at the expense of 'responsibility'.

The remedy advanced by Baggini is a return to ethics and the displacement of legalism as the dominant moral framework: 'The grievance culture is a weed which has driven out its fairer relative – moral complaint. There are other ways of trying to prune it, but if we want to attack it at its roots, we need the soil of ethics, not law' (Baggini, 2008: 125). Such a return entails the recognition that 'moral discourse is democratic, rational activity', at its centre the weighing of reasons and the democratic practice of reasoned deliberation in a context of pluralistic value. The necessary pre-condition for the art of complaining is civic education, not just in classrooms but on 'the street', where citizens gain first-hand experience of democratic deliberation and agency in their daily encounters with the state and with other citizens who work for it in its most mundane but powerful manifestation.

Baggini's invitation is to the reclaiming of complaint for the 'forces of progress' and its rescue from the snares of 'wrong complaint', which variously assumes contradictory, self-defeating, self-serving, nostalgic, misdirected, conformist, empty and sometimes ostensibly paranoid form. It is 'wrong complaint' of this sort that is manifest in a culture which 'undermines ethics and replaces it with a legalistic set of attitudes which undermines responsibility, freedom, and a proper sense of life's contingencies' (Baggini, 2008: 127). Cultivation of the art of complaining is not therefore simply a matter of learning how to fill out an application form more accurately, cite more relevant examples, quantify loss or construct a case more persuasively by adopting a more appropriate tone and style (although all these skills might well be useful). It is instead an aspect of the wider art of citizenship that recognizes that to use a public service 'is to take part in a shared endeavour: my child's school, my ailment, my university fees, potholes in my street, bobbies on the beat – all these come at an opportunity cost to others' (Toynbee and Walker, 2017: 307). Complaints can indeed be a gift if deployed as an instrument of democratic learning and problem-solving, not as a weapon. To be so, they must form part of the way in which citizens address the 'rationing choices' that inevitably accompany participation and cooperation in the difficult decisions to be made about the public resources collectively owned. The counterpart of the citizen-agency of street-level bureaucrats is in other words the citizen-agency of all citizens themselves.

Repressive, autonomous and responsive legalities

What follows in later chapters does not seek to displace legal categories entirely, although a critique of liberal legalism will be central to the argument advanced. Instead, it will be suggested that contemporary legalism can be situated within a broader scheme of legalities which comprises the 'repressive', the 'autonomous' and the 'responsive'. That scheme owes its origins to a short but visionary work by two socio-legal authors in the pragmatist tradition of American legal realism, Philippe Nonet and Philip Selznick, who were based at the pioneering Centre for the Study of Law and Society, University of California at Berkeley (Nonet and Selznick, 2001). Published in 1978 but conceived during the convulsive years of the previous decade, *Toward Responsive Law* aimed ambitiously to reintegrate legal, political and social theory by recasting jurisprudential issues in a social scientific perspective. More specifically, Nonet and Selznick sought to analyse and assess different forms of legal ordering according to a typology that incorporates political and jurisprudential aspects of law, and by doing so to address directly the role of law in contemporary democracies.

A 'repressive' legal order, they propose, is one in which the courts are closely identified with, and in the direct service of, the executive state, with the overarching aim of 'keeping the peace' and promoting security. Legal institutions accordingly have few resources other than the coercive power afforded them by the state itself, their central concern and mode of authority residing primarily in the criminal law. Under a regime of repressive legality, legal rules are highly visible, their implementation by the state granted an almost unrestricted measure of discretion counterbalanced by only the most precarious recognition of rights.

An 'autonomous' legal order by contrast is diligent in separating law from politics and the state, with the separation of legislative and judicial functions marked emphatically. As in the case of repressive law, rules are notably prominent in an autonomous legal order, as a means of ensuring legal accountability on the part of the state bureaucracy and limiting official discretion. The focus is as a result on procedural rather than substantive justice, legal competence demonstrated by qualities of regularity and fairness. Strict obedience to the rules of positive law is celebrated, and any deviation or even criticism taken as a sign of civic infidelity. If autonomous legality sounds familiar, it is because it represents most closely the form of legality that has prevailed in most contemporary liberal democracies and as a result seems the most authentic and 'natural' option.

By contrast, 'responsive' law, viewed by the authors as singularly appropriate to modern conditions, valorizes overarching 'purpose' in legal reasoning at the expense of the 'artificial reason of law'. The primacy of 'purpose' entails the relaxation of claims to law's sovereignty and enables a 'less rigid and more civil conception' of public order by accentuating the notions of citizenship, dispersed authority and responsibility. As law becomes more open and flexible through a subtle interplay of rules and principle, so social advocacy, and its associated modes of participation, assumes a more political aspect, seeking to reform and improve legal institutions. The test of legal institutions is no longer that of sovereignty, adherence to the rules or 'justice as fairness', but rather 'competence' in achieving purpose that is beyond law and legality. As a result, the 'rule of law' model of autonomous legality is stretched beyond its limits to accommodate the affirmation of public purpose, with claims based on rights recognized not as ends in themselves but as opportunities for disclosing systemic malfunction and as constructive sources of administrative intelligence. In such a context, the priority is the pragmatist one of identifying systemic problems and their structural remedy (Nonet and Selznick, 2001: 106).

The argument advanced in later chapters is that postliberal politics entails a regulatory mode of engaging with citizen grievance that is 'responsive', in the sense proposed by Nonet and Selznick (and advanced in different form by Zach Richards' revival of Nonet and Selznick's insights, *Responsive Legality: The New Administrative Justice* [2019]). That conclusion follows from the recognition that neither repressive nor autonomous law can accommodate the complexities of contemporary democratic pluralism, nor the forms of street-level bureaucracy disclosed by ethnographic enquiry. More specifically, while responsive law, like autonomous law, retains as its 'master ideal' a definite form of legality, it resists the tendency towards legalism to which autonomous law is prone with its 'proliferation of rules and procedural formalities' (Nonet and Selznick, 2001: 108). Instead, responsive law is a search for a regulatory system that extends beyond proceduralism and formalism, fairness and regularity, to substantive justice and to institutions that are 'competent': 'If there is a paradigmatic function of responsive law, it is regulation, not adjudication', 'regulation' in turn being conceived as a 'mechanism for clarifying the public interest', or common good (Nonet and Selznick, 2001: 108).

3

The 'Social Imaginary' of Liberal Legalism

Autonomous legality and the liberal legalism into which it habitually elides represent more than a method, a way of proceeding or a set of techniques. Instead, they have to them an imaginative dimension that establishes a distinctive mentality, which through social reinforcement comes to seem mere common sense. It is this quality of liberal legalism that inspires its potency and its manifestation in subtly different guises, whether those of the common law mind, rights-based legalism or constitutionalism. In the image of the judge, also capable of deployment in the cause of a more repressive alternative, autonomous legality, and its sibling liberal legalism, finds persuasive expression.

The limits of liberal legalism

'A pathology of the legal order'

In a study of the California Industrial Accident Commission (IAC) published in 1969, sociologist Philippe Nonet turned his attention to a government agency with significant dispute-resolution and rights-determining functions. Its remit was the administration of workers' compensation laws in California, which since 1910 had governed the liability of employers for injuries to employees at work. The story Nonet had to tell was one of 'the transformation of a welfare agency into a court of law', of how an administrative authority with wide discretion and a mandate for social action had during the course of 50 years 'lost most of its early sense of initiative and public mission', instead acquiring the 'outlook of a passive arbitrator, responsible only to those private interests of labor and industry it was originally meant to regulate' (Nonet, 1969: 1). The story was, in other words, one of 'legalization', whereby the IAC became a 'highly self-conscious judicial body, largely removed from the concrete problems of welfare policy and governed by exacting standards of procedure' (Nonet, 1969: 1).

A significant aspect of the process of transition identified by Nonet was what he described as the gradual shift from 'pattern orientation' to 'claims orientation'. In its early days, the IAC had little interest in the adjudication of individual claims. Instead, its chief concern was to create or foster appropriate practices in the management of claims and the provision of medical care, with interventions limited in purpose to educational and corrective action. In that context, the IAC's residual adjudicative functions were merely a 'safety valve' for the small minority of cases that did not resolve themselves. As Nonet summarized the position, '[t]he concerns of the commission were for patterns governing the private administration of benefits; the actions it contemplated were of a corrective rather than remedial character' (Nonet, 1969: 157).

In a climate of increasing tension in industrial relations, the IAC found itself over time seeking protection from conflict by focusing on individual claims and problems, and thereby disentangling itself from political controversy: '[T]he case-by-case approach served as a means of atomizing group demands and stripping the debate of the political character it increasingly tended to assume' (Nonet, 1969: 157). This policy of self-protection ultimately proved unsuccessful and, in the process, entailed significant cost: '[I]nstead of promoting reforms of structure through regulation or the advocacy of new legislation, the agency would limit its competence to the provision of remedies in cases of inadequate compliance with compensation policies' (Nonet, 1969: 157). The purposive pursuit of public welfare and the common good became submerged in the handling of disaggregated and compartmentalized individual claims, the IAC being forced to retreat into an enduring 'posture of aloof and blind impartiality' (Nonet, 1969: 158). As Nonet concludes:

> With its focus on individual remedies, rather than on correcting patterns of action, the IAC has lost sensitivity and responsiveness to the systematic conditions affecting its work … Having vested all its energies in the one-by-one determination of claims, the agency has lost its competence to deal with the conditions and the systematic patterns in which those claims are produced. (Nonet, 1969: 159)

This shift in focus from the promotion of public welfare to the adjudication of individual disputes was part of what Nonet identified as a broader process of legalization and judicialization. Legalization he characterized as the growth of the role of law in practical problem-solving and the elaboration of legal rules and doctrines, dependent in turn on a system of procedures and modes of reasoning which serve as vehicles for the use and elaboration of law (Nonet, 1969: 2). Judicialization was apparent in the gradual accretion to the IAC and its officials of the style and approach of a judge to this realization of legality, with an originally administrative function being transformed into one of adjudication (Nonet, 1969: 165–201). The distinction between administration and adjudication is that between an activity that 'looks to the end-in-view, the refashioning of human or other resources so that a particular outcome will be achieved', and one that seeks instead to 'realise the ideals of legality' (Nonet, 1969: 247). The purpose of administration is 'not justice but accomplishment, not fairness but therapy', while the task of adjudication is discovery of the 'legal co-ordinates of a particular situation' (Nonet, 1969: 247).

Nonet's account is an invitation not so much to the jettisoning of legality in its entirety but rather for the moderation of the claims made for a particular style of legality. His primary critique of the IAC is not that it increasingly found a place for law in its practice but that in doing so it opted for a 'restrictive' and 'conventional' approach to law which confined it to a system of judicialization, comprising adjudication on the application of rules by increasingly court-like structures. Such a restricted approach was at the expense of a more 'generic' conception of law which recognizes legality as serving broader public value and contributing to 'civic competence' and citizenship (Nonet, 1969: 2–3). The IAC had, in other words, succumbed to that 'pathology of the legal order' that is captured by its designation as 'legalism', as an insistence on legal rules or modes of reasoning even when they frustrate rather than affirm public policy (Nonet, 1969: 265). In that case, law becomes an abstraction, something rigid and incapable of responding to actual needs. Legalism in effect brings law into disrepute, inviting the sort of alienation from its mandate that legal consciousness scholars identify among street-level bureaucrats whose patience with the law finally runs out. For Nonet, 'legalism is an issue about the competence of the law as an instrument of problem-solving', whereby the limitations of restrictive notions of legality become all too apparent in their inability to respond to changing social circumstance (Nonet, 1969: 265).

In Britain, an interested reader of Nonet's work was Richard Titmuss, one of the architects of the welfare state. Citing Nonet's study, Titmuss wrote with some prescience of his fear that 'the pathology of legalism' was in danger of debilitating the democratic foundations of the postwar settlement (Titmuss, 1971). By legalism, he meant an 'insistence on legal rules based on precedent and responsive only very slowly to rapidly changing human needs and circumstances' (Titmuss, 1971: 124–5). The source of such a mentality he found in the work of A.V. Dicey, the 19th-century jurist who had pre-eminently warned against the encroachment of administrative discretion on the freedom of the individual and its threat to the protections afforded by the domestic judge-made common law. The primary contemporary culprits identified by Titmuss as the 'new Diceyists' were those who, taking contemporary inspiration from economist Milton Friedman and the Chicago

School, sought to achieve more individual freedom, both civic and market, through less government and less bureaucracy. Reinforcing the role of courts would have the effect desired by these new Diceyists of reducing that of 'lay people' in dispute and complaint procedures and thereby of marginalizing the 'amateurish, inquisitorial and moralising' participation of ordinary citizens (Titmuss, 1971, 115).

Less predictable, thought Titmuss, was the contemporary alignment with the new Diceyists of a new breed of 'left legalists', who, in emulation of US-style civil rights cause-lawyering, had promoted the pursuit of minority rights through litigation as part of 'the more general protest and liberation movement' (Titmuss, 1971: 117; Brown and Halley, 2002b). In the US, the perceived 'tyrannies of the so-called bureaucrat of the public welfare system' had in this way been challenged by a 'populist' strategy of more lawyers, more legal process and more case law to establish authoritative precedent (Titmuss, 1971: 118). This new 'access to justice movement', based on the assertion of individual rights and judicialized appeal systems, rested, thought Titmuss, upon a number of false assumptions: that justice will be advanced inevitably 'if case law is substituted for administrative decision; if all appeal systems are judicialized and claimants are represented by lawyers; if all discretionary cash additions are abolished; if access to the courts is made available to all claimants, and if the adversary system replaces the inquisitorial lay tribunal' (Titmuss, 1971: 118). Underlying such assumptions rested a 'quaint belief in the mechanistic objectivity of lawyer's law and the impartiality of judges' (Titmuss, 1971: 119). More insidious, however, was a creeping individualism that threatened to undermine the public welfare and common good. For it was far from clear, argued Titmuss, that this form of judicialization benefitted public assistance claimants collectively, rather than just a sequence of single lone claimants: the more 'legal' such processes become, the more the broader aims of social welfare programmes are frustrated by 'case law, legal mystification and a litigious courthouse atmosphere' (Titmuss, 1971: 122).

The 'misapplication of juristic distinctions'

Such insights, stirred by Titmuss' reading of Nonet's study and forged in his engagement in the practical politics of the first decades of the British welfare state, resonate with the thought of US political theorist Judith Shklar, whose more systematic reflections on the implications of legalistic ideology for political theorists had started to appear in the mid-1960s. As Shklar sought to demonstrate, legalism, as both the practical ethos of lawyers and as a political ideology, is at root 'the ethical attitude that holds moral conduct to be a matter of rule following, and moral relationships to consist of duties and rights determined by rules' (Shklar, 1986: 1). Although legalism constitutes the professional ethos of the legal profession, as a political ideology and source of practice it is far from confined to lawyers. On the contrary, legalism, with the courtroom and 'tribunality' as its model, shapes 'legislative assemblies, bureaucracies, and mediations of all kinds'. Legalism is not merely an article of constitutional principle or an assertion of public law theory; it is instead a climate of opinion, a mentality or, as Shklar argued, the pervasive ideology of contemporary liberal states. Citing the 'felicitous phrase' of American jurist Lon Fuller, Shklar identifies the chief difficulty with legalism as its tendency towards 'the misapplication of juristic distinctions to a context that will not support them' (Shklar, 1966: 51). By asserting the law's autonomy and separation from political and social context, legalism makes a fetish of 'the law' as abstraction that is unsustainable in the face of democratic pluralism and diversity.

As Shklar also argued, the practices of legalism are frequently counter-productive in such a political context, court-like procedures easily serving 'to make people more intransigent, less capable of living with each other' (Shklar, 1966: 54). While 'arbitration' may well be 'the butt of lawyerly contempt', it is nevertheless apparent that 'adjudication is not the path to conciliation' (Shklar, 1966: 57). Legalism, at its worst when insisting on an 'uncompromising policy of judicialization', and for all its pretensions to 'responsiveness to social changes', remains a 'conservatizing influence' (Shklar, 1966: 57).

The pursuit of 'pure' law founders on its lack of social realism, its failure to acknowledge law as just one among many social forces. Yet for Shklar, the consequence of her critique is not that of undermining laws and legal institutions. Laws and legal institutions are not for Shklar 'the chief ideological screen behind which shameless liberalism hides', as claimed by some (Shklar, 1987: 10). To be critical of legalism as an extreme and perverse version of legality is, for Shklar, neither to jettison liberalism nor reject as one of its legitimate components a form of 'rule of law' that can serve as 'a more effective social force, a more intelligible and defensible political ideology, and a more useful concept in social theory' (Shklar, 1966: 58). Shklar's critique is to that extent a prescription not of a post-legal utopia but of a post-legalistic rehabilitation of the rule of law. Any such rehabilitation entails, however, due recognition of a meaningfully democratic context as a necessary precondition, and of the place of law as one element on a spectrum of social and political forces rather than an abstracted and autonomous sphere of influence. Insofar as liberalism enshrines a form of legality, it must not, in Shklar's view, look to 'the liberalism of the "rule of law" ideal promoted by Friedrich von Hayek and his followers', both conservative and radically egalitarian, but to a form of liberal democracy in which the democratic limb has at least as much strength as the liberal limb (Shklar, 1986: xi).

The faces of liberal legalism

The 'American style of law' and Euro-legalism

The nature and expansion of a US style of legalism that is notably 'adversarial' has remained subject to sustained and critical examination since the salvos of Shklar and Titmuss. Such critique acknowledges the objective and not inconsiderable achievements of legalism, notably, for example, in improving incrementally the situations of socially disadvantaged groups. In short, legalism has been used successfully as a tool to constrain 'racist attitudes, repressive moralism or bureaucratic callousness', especially when trust between citizens and state has been in short supply or broken down entirely (Kagan, 2001: 163–4). Yet such successes come at a price. That price is apparent most obviously in the limited ability of legalism to achieve remedies that are substantive and more than merely procedural. While making government more responsive to individualized claims, adversarial legalism emerges as nevertheless deeply flawed, 'a peculiarly cumbersome, erratic, costly and often ineffective method of policy implementation and dispute resolution' (Kagan, 2001: 164).

Notwithstanding such serious limitations, this 'American way of law' has been transplanted successfully elsewhere. Throughout much of Europe, in discrete fields, such as securities regulation, competition law and disability rights, a process of 'juridification' has reflected the easy affinity between the advocacy of individual rights and the quest for centralized legitimacy. In practice, this process has led to increased legislation of judicially enforceable legal rights and norms, 'access to justice' reforms for private parties, increases in levels of litigation and notable expansion of the legal services industry within the 'European area of justice'. Such 'Euro-legalism' is illustrated by a marked increase in the number of practising lawyers, growth of the legal insurance market, expansion in the size of law firms and inflation of the overall market value of the 'legal services industry' (Keleman, 2011: 240).

As in the US, so in Europe the rise of a distinctly adversarial form of legalism has not been without its notable benefits: new substantive rights, increased transparency, legal certainty and 'access to justice', albeit waxing and waning, especially in nation states where these characteristics were previously absent or in limited supply. At the same time, in much the same way as in the US, such benefits have come at a price: the diminished credibility of elected representatives; the marginalization of citizen participation; the undermining of the traditional European consensus model of democracy; a huge increase in the burden imposed on often precarious court structures; and, above all, the prioritization of individual rights over the broader public interest or common good (Keleman, 2011).

'Modern constitutionalism' and the retreat from politics

This enlargement of the range of legalism is symbiotic with the project of modern constitutionalism that has witnessed, globally, the emergence of constitution-making as the preferred route to social justice, with entrenched rights and judicial review the vehicle of choice for its realization (Moyn, 2010, 2018). The Canadian Charter of Rights and Freedoms 1982, the New Zealand Bill of Rights Act 1990, the Israeli Basic Laws 1992 and the South African Bill of Rights 1996 (and creation of a new Constitutional Court in 1995) were significant early landmarks in a process that gathered pace most notably in the period after the collapse of the Soviet Union.

The widely held belief that the entrenchment of constitutional rights and their protection by the courts is a progressive and redistributive development has nevertheless suffered significant disillusionment (Moyn, 2018). Even before the most recent wave of critical analysis, a study of the impact of early constitutionalism in Canada, New Zealand, Israel and South Africa concluded that there is a stark contrast between 'the limited impact of constitutionalism on enhancing the life conditions of the have-nots' and its 'significant contribution to the removal of so-called market rigidities and the promotion of economic liberties' (Hirschl, 2004: 14). While the creation of individual constitutional rights may serve the interests of 'negative liberty', which relies on procedural fairness and non-interference, it is far from clear it assists significantly in the promotion of positive liberty in the form of social rights, enhanced human capability or the creation of more egalitarian societies. What the study's author describes as 'the well-orchestrated judicial empowerment game' emerges as a global trend whereby 'policy-making authority is increasingly transferred by hegemonic elites from majoritarian policy-making arenas to semi-autonomous professional policy-making bodies primarily in order to insulate their policy preferences from the vicissitudes of democratic politics' (Hirschl, 2004: 16).

The advance of legalism, like that of modern constitutionalism, can be read convincingly, in other words, as a retreat from politics, or, more specifically, from democratic politics (Crick, 1962; Mouffe, 1993). The distinctive form of liberalism, or neoliberalism, that has gained ascendancy since 1979, and more particularly in a global context since 1989, is marked by a legalistic strain that reveals its jurisprudential underpinning. 'Liberal legalism' emerges as the house philosophy of the neoliberal state, the 'apotheosis' of the rule of law as 'the law of rules' (Loughlin, 2018) and 'the misrule of lawyers' (Anderson, 2021: 31), accompanied by subservience over time to a form of 'cosmopolitan constitutionalism' that depends on the 'invisible constitution' and a set of universal principles determined increasingly by transnational judicial agencies (Somek, 2014; Loughlin, 2022). Among the identified progenitors of that philosophy, notably Rawls and Dworkin, Nozick and Hayek, are philosophical legalists of both egalitarian and more libertarian persuasion. According to their critics, and despite their substantive differences, all share a fundamental belief that principles of justice and rights can be formulated that are both 'highly determinate' and 'ideally universal'. Insofar as they disagree, they do so not from different positions in the philosophy of law but from 'antagonistic conceptions of the good life' that are essentially political in character. Their appeal to justice and rights marginalizes political disagreement about ends, thereby claiming to circumvent any residual conflict about the good. In the case of both libertarian and egalitarian forms of liberal legalism, the central institution is not so much a deliberative assembly or parliament as a court of law capable of conducting a process of adjudication that is marked by proceduralism and formalism, whatever its substantive deficiencies (Gray, 2000: 19).

Common law revivalism: an 'enchanted landscape'

It is the translation of liberal legalism into customary practice that enables it to exercise such tenacious hold over modern public institutions. So pervasive are its assumptions and its ways of proceeding that it seems almost 'natural', an inevitable part of the human response to social and political complexity. It takes a determined effort of the imagination to reassert the contested and invented quality of 'law'. Yet legal history invites such re-imagining, serving as a reminder that western modes of autonomous legality are neither timeless nor universal: 'Law is a social and mental form that has invaded modernity, quickly becoming an essential component of our lives', but, crucially, in 'a form invented by the ancient Romans'; in the ancient Greek world, as in Confucian China, the idea of an autonomous legal sphere, with its own habits of mind, conceptual framework and professional caste, was largely unknown (Schiavone, 2012: 3).

In Britain in particular, there is moreover an implicit understanding that 'law' is somehow part of the national identity, synonymous with a distinctive form of liberty and ancient constitution. Neither the intrusion of modernity nor its US-style vehicle has been necessary for it to flourish. Indeed, for a certain type of nostalgic conservatism, the common law assumes almost sacred status as the protector of home and hearth, a place that is 'ours', that is 'safe, law-governed and protected', nothing less in fact than an 'enchanted landscape': 'The common law has stood like a shield between the individual and the sovereign power; it has always enjoyed a higher authority than the decrees of politicians for the simple reason that it is by virtue of the common law that the politicians hold office' (Scruton, 2002: 25, 50).

It should not be supposed that the romance of the common law has faded into ancient history, to be replaced by a more 'vibrant, decent, reformed common law, one that disowns its own murky past while being (in some complicated way) rooted in it' (Gearty, 2016: 31). On the contrary, it has been observed that there is abroad among England's green pastures a 'new mood of common law revivalism' that has extended into politics as well as the higher echelons of the judiciary (Gearty, 2016: 19). Dicey's vision of the 'law state' which underpins such romanticism and in which the Bar and the judiciary are the heroes of a distinctively British style of liberty, individuality, self-help and entrepreneurship has been theorized as a form of normativism that reifies 'the rule of law' as part of a judge-made constitution built on case law and individual rights induced from 'the ordinary law of the land' (Loughlin, 1992). At the root of Dicey's concept of the rule of law lies a form of classical liberalism that has easily coalesced with more contemporary forms of neoliberalism to achieve hegemonic status.

Liberal-legalist understandings and practices

Behind these various faces of liberal legalism rests what Taylor calls a 'social imaginary', which is more than just a theory or intellectual scheme. Instead, a social imaginary of this sort is made up of 'the ways people imagine their social existence, how they fit together with others, how things go on between them and their fellows, the expectations that are normally met, and the deeper normative notions and images that underlie these expectations' (Taylor, 2004: 23). Such a social imaginary comprises a mixture of 'background understandings', or expectations, and 'practices', or practical ways of proceeding. The legalistic social imaginary is most apparent not so much in the explicit statement of theoretical positions but through its implicit acceptance in taken-for-granted modes of practice, not just by professional lawyers but by decision-makers and citizens in everyday life.

An overview of the 'background understandings' and 'practices' comprising liberal legalism has been offered by US jurist W.H. Simon from within the pragmatist tradition of legal realism (Simon, 2004). According to Simon, three basic assumptions or understandings inform the practices deemed to be fair under a dispensation that combines liberalism with legalism. First, there is the understanding that the plight of an aggrieved citizen should be interpreted primarily as one of potential victimhood. This 'victim perspective' is one which routinely concentrates attention on plaintiffs, consumers and complainants as atomized individuals, uprooted from any social context, and to the exclusion of shared situations and interdependencies. Secondly, there is an understanding in favour of a 'populist mistrust' of large organizations, whether governmental or commercial, and suspicion that all such institutions are inefficient, unfair and corruptible, even if not wilfully corrupt. This populist perspective is inclined to focus in an administrative context on the individual as 'underdog', as a passive victim of an alienating and antagonistic state bureaucracy, which invariably tramples over all personal expressions of subjectivity, with little room for acknowledgement of any possible alliance of interests between state and individual. Thirdly, there is an understanding that 'individual rights are trumps' over all other values, including that of the common good. The rights in question are exclusively individualistic and libertarian, with an emphasis on 'choice' and 'privacy' as expressions of autonomy. To yield ground from such primacy of individual rights is seen as flirtation with agonistic politics. Such a focus is highly sensitive to distinguishing characteristics, reluctant to let extraneous context intrude on the singularity of the matter under consideration, and in retreat from any shared social or collective perspective that might bring to bear values other than those expressed in the language of individual entitlement. This is an emphasis which excludes any mediating institutions, pitching the alienating state against the alienated individual without the benefit of social intermediaries to soften the blow. It entails a space that is linear and simple, devoid of the complexity afforded by the insertion between state and individual of civic association – a simple space that denies pluralism, whether of shared values or identity.

In addition to these dominant understandings of victimhood, populism and individual rights, Simon identifies liberalism of a legalist character as importing three characteristic practices or ways of proceeding. First, 'procedural individuation and differentiation' reduces any common, shared or clustered concerns to a single issue, associated with a single individual, and encapsulated in a single 'case' whereby any commonality, shared perspective or public benefit is marginalized. Adjudication emerges as the defining practice for enforcing individual rights and the judicial trial as the ideal type of such adjudicatory practice, scrupulously differentiated from the ordinary practice of administration. Secondly, there is a celebration of 'enforceable rules as norms', with scant regard for the exercise of discretion, which is in turn identified as a form of deviance to be avoided or at least contained as far as possible. In the event of contravention, monetary compensation is the preferred medium of redress, with individual 'closure' and 'business as usual' the most prized conclusion to proceedings. Thirdly, 'bilateral control of information' is ceded to the parties to an individual dispute with consequent emphasis on secrecy until the eventual drama of oral testimony. Under such a rubric, adversarial combat, and the theoretical promise, albeit quite rarely realized in practice, of the one-off adversarial trial are consolidated as the ideal response (Simon, 2004).

Liberal legalism and autonomous law

Judge-made law and 'cosmopolitan constitutionalism'

To move beyond this everyday habituation of liberal legalism and situate it in a broader theoretical scheme is to acknowledge both the achievements and limitations of background understandings that privilege victim perspective, populism and 'rights as trumps', and ways of proceeding shaped by procedural individuation and differentiation, 'rules as norms' and bilateral control of information. For Dicey, the 'high priest of orthodox constitutional theory' (Loughlin, 1992: 140), the veneration of the common law courts and the rule of law, narrowly conceived as judge-made law, expressed the valorization of individual liberty, suspicion of the state and support of limited government. It was a short step from suggesting that the courts are the only defence of individual liberty against the state to saying that the courts are the only effective guardians against the perceived evils of state socialism (Loughlin, 1992: 161). The history of that judicial guardianship was the subject of J.A.G. Griffith's *The Politics of the Judiciary* (Griffith, 1977), which so shaped a whole generation of lawyers' perception of the role of the judiciary as serving the forces of conservatism in British political life. For a later, more liberally minded generation, the tables were turned, and, not without some irony, the judges came to be seen as the liberal protectors of individual rights from governments of decidedly non-socialistic disposition. Taking inspiration from the legalistic and rationalistic approaches to political philosophy of Rawls' and Dworkin's rights-based liberalism, this liberal legalism has 'transformed law from precedent or instrument into a general moral concept requiring fidelity not just to rules but to the principles of fairness and justice that legal rules presuppose' (Loughlin, 2019: 18). At its centre, liberal jurisprudence has exposed principles of proportionality, legal certainty, consistency and respect for fundamental, and mainly libertarian, human rights. It has also entailed the reformulation of the rule of law as the rule of rights as much as the rule of rules, to serve as a 'tool of modernisation and development' (Loughlin, 2018: 665).

Such principles are also at the heart of modern constitutionalism with its similar reverence for a particular rights-based conception of the rule of law and for the constitution, written or unwritten, as the primary source of legal and political principle. The constitution, under the guardianship of an unelected judiciary, can be relied upon to protect individual rights and fundamental freedoms (including market freedom), modern 'cosmopolitan constitutionalism' (Somek, 2014) emerging as a form of 'civil religion' (Loughlin, 2022).

Autonomous legality and 'the artificial reason' of law

The chief characteristic of such approaches, advanced, for example, by jurists T.R.S. Allan and Jeffrey Jowell (Tomkins, 2005: 12), is the embrace of law as an autonomous field, separate from and superior to politics and society. Drawing a bold line between legislative and judicial functions, autonomous law celebrates its control over public agencies and upholds a measure of accountability based on a system of rules to rein in officialdom and of rights to protect the individual citizen. Its characteristic devices for exercising control are formalism and procedural fairness rather than substantive justice, its mode of operation an impersonal and 'mechanical' style of adjudication which successfully depoliticizes disputes and seeks resolution by focusing on the individual case rather than any broader context of social conflict. Its practitioners are valued technicians and manipulators of the legal process and of its 'artificial reason' (Nonet and Selznick, 2001).

Close accountability to rules and principle is the abiding virtue of autonomous law. When set against the unaccountable and arbitrary exercise of sovereign power which it sought to restrain, such virtue is of estimable and compelling benefit. An alternative dispensation that makes legal institutions permeable to political power and identifies them closely with the state makes for authoritarian rule and prioritization of the 'official' point of view that lends administrative convenience the upper hand. The characterization of such legal regimes as 'repressive' effectively evokes the contrast with a more liberal and autonomous form of legality. Nevertheless, if accountability to rule and principle is the virtue of autonomous legality, too close an association with such forces yields its vicious propensity to legalism and the deformation of its characteristic strengths. Due process and Rawlsian 'justice as fairness' entail a scrupulous observance of rules of standing that limit access, emphasize the initiative and responsibility of individual parties, encode strict criteria of evidential relevance, confine judicial attention to the case in hand, and valorize forms of judicial reasoning that are abstract, 'neutral' and impervious to substantive outcomes. This 'rule of law' model of justice brings with it the benefits of judicial autonomy but at the same time significantly limits the capacity of the legal process to respond to changing social circumstance and engage in effective problem-solving.

Legalistic imaginaries: *The Judge*

Siegfried Charoux and George Orwell

The symbolic iconography of 'the judge' is indicative of the sort of legalism, repressive or autonomous, that any alternative legality would need to transfigure. In the Royal Courts of Justice (RCJ) in central London there is a sculpture aptly called *The Judge*, situated at the entrance to the modern

Queen's Building, an annex to the imposing 19th-century Gothic cathedral of justice that presents its awe-inspiring judicial face to the world on the Strand. The route through the central Neo-Gothic hall of the main RCJ building, with its imposing structure, its portraits and its statues of celebrated Victorian lawyers, leads eventually to *The Judge* situated before an open courtyard. Unlike the judicial images that adorn the central hall, *The Judge* is entirely anonymous, faceless and impersonal. It is an effigy of the judicial officeholder as dehumanized abstraction, like an armoured *Star Wars* warrior, bewigged, robed and cuffed, rippling with masculine musculature and forbidding man-spread (Royal Academy, 1963: 55; Chamot et al, 1964; Veasey, 2019).

The Judge is the work of Austrian émigré sculptor Siegfried Charoux, who fled Vienna in 1935, and whose work *The Islanders* was exhibited at the Festival of Britain in 1951. *The Judge* was commissioned by Gerald Gardiner (whose involvement with the campaigning law reform group Justice and its support of the first UK Parliamentary Commissioner or 'Ombudsman' is notable, Gardiner's wife and biographer, Muriel Box, even referring to the Parliamentary Commissioner Bill as 'Gerald's Bill' [Box, 1983: 190]) and completed in 1962 before finding its resting place in the reception area of the Queen's Building opened by Queen Elizabeth II in 1968. Although *The Judge* is considered part of a *Civilization Cycle* of sculptures by Charoux, which include other public works such as *The Motorcyclist* (1957) and *The Cellist* (1959), and which also have affinities with Charoux's other work of the period, such as *The Neighbours* (1959), *The Commuter* (1960) and *The Poet* (1962), it is quite different in tone and feel, a striking contrast to the other depictions of civilization which find its chief virtues residing in ordinary citizens and their everyday activity.

Charoux observed of *The Judge* that it 'represents Justice (jurisprudence and jurisdiction) in that inhuman form mankind all over the world now tolerates: drapery and an obsession for punishment' (Chamot et al, 1964: 99). It is a representation that evokes the majesty of the law, its 'assertive power' (Veasey, 2019) and austerity. It evokes also the observation on the English judge in the celebrated essay *The Lion and the Unicorn* by George Orwell, friend and correspondent of Charoux, as 'that typically English figure, the hanging judge, some gouty old bully with his mind rooted in the nineteenth century, handing out savage sentences'; he is an 'evil old man in scarlet robe and horse-hair wig, whom nothing short of dynamite will ever teach what century he is living in, but who will at any rate interpret the law according to the books and will in no circumstances take a money bribe'; he is one of the symbolic figures of England, of the 'strange mixture of reality and illusion, democracy and privilege, humbug and decency, the subtle network of compromises, by which the nation keeps itself in its familiar shape' (Orwell, 1941: 87–8).

As the context indicates, Orwell has in mind the criminal law judge, and indeed it is the symbolism of the criminal law that perhaps best captures the tone of repressive law and its rigorous promulgation of a distinctive style of 'rule of law'. Orwell's ambivalence and grudging acknowledgement of the value of the hanging judge as a desirable and necessary alternative to 'the Nazi storm trooper' is that of Charoux's sculpture as well. As Orwell recognizes, somewhat incongruously in the spirit of Dicey, 'Here one comes upon an all-important English trait: the respect for constitutionalism and legality, the belief in "the law" as something above the State and above the individual, something which is cruel and stupid, of course, but at any rate incorruptible' (Orwell, 1941: 85–6).

Ian McEwan: The Children Act

Charoux's sculpture makes a brief yet provocative appearance in the film of Ian McEwan's novel, *The Children Act* (McEwan, 2014), in which Emma Thompson plays Lady Fiona Maye, a High Court judge in the Family Division. As McEwan acknowledges, the novel owes much to Court of Appeal judge Sir Alan Ward, "a judge of great wisdom, wit and humanity". The novel's unfolding narrative is concerned with Lady Maye's own humanity and its interaction with the requirements of the law. She is depicted as efficient, crisp and professionally detached, a refined connoisseur of Bach, Mahler and Schubert, a purveyor of 'elegant and correct' judgments. Yet she is compassionate and humane, regretting to some extent the passing of 'the old system' which although 'slow and inefficient' had preserved 'the human touch' in a way that the judicial modernization programme discounted, with its tick-boxes and the lives of children 'held in computer memory, accurately, but rather less kindly' (McEwan, 2014: 36). She recognizes too with Dickensian flourish the ill-fitting quality of the relationship between law and life, the at times 'absurdity and pointlessness' of her involvement as a judge in a situation which should have been 'handed to a social worker, who could have taken half an hour to reach a sensible decision', but which is instead 'transmuted into a monstrous clerical task, into box-files of legal documents so numerous and heavy they were hauled to court on trolleys, into hours of educational wrangling, procedural hearings, deferred decisions, the whole circus rising, but so slowly, through the judicial hierarchy like a lopsided, ill-tethered hot-air balloon' (McEwan, 2014: 36).

That separation of public and private, professional and personal, holds good until those separate worlds collide in a case concerning an 'end of life decision' about a young man whose parents, Jehovah's Witnesses, wish him to refrain from a life-saving blood transfusion. In the film, Charoux's alarming sculpture can be seen looming behind the young man's family as they gather before the hearing of the hospital's application to perform the transfusion. It offers a counterpoint to the modern liberal judge represented by Lady Maye and portrayed as such by Emma Thompson, a judge for whom the search for legal principle, not legal rules, is paramount:

> Quoting Lord Justice Ward, Fiona reminded all parties in the opening lines of her judgment, 'This court is a court of law, not of morals, and our task has been to find, and our duty is then to apply, the relevant principles of law to the situation before us – a situation which is unique.' (McEwan, 2014: 26–7)

In these various evocations of the symbolism of the law and its presence in national life, Charoux, Orwell and McEwan summon the separate but conversing spirits of repressive and autonomous legality, over whom the ghost of Dicey lingers and an overarching ideology of legalism presides.

4

The Promise of Postliberalism

The association of contemporary liberalism with a legalistic social imaginary makes urgent the task of renewed critique in an era that is characterized as postliberal. Postliberalism as a political stance entails reacquaintance with strands of liberal thought that have slipped from prominence. In particular, it seeks to recognize the state as positive and ethical, and to situate the individual in a complex web of civic association that is a source of both identity and political agency. In the tradition of political pragmatism, it finds a function for response to citizen grievance that is primarily problem-solving and consensus-building rather than adjudicatory. Its imaginative representation, in contrast to that of the judge, resituates the virtue of justice in the company of other virtuous dispositions and as an aspect of the common good.

Postliberal democracy: 'going on together'

Warnings of liberalism's demise are hardly new, and indeed the concept of postliberalism by now has a significant pedigree (Gray, 1993). Various forms of communitarian, civic-republican or radical-democratic glosses on liberal themes are well established, including experiments in Third Way and Big Society politics. Indeed, the New Liberalism of L. T. Hobhouse and J. A. Hobson, which in the years before the First World War responded to the new wave of interventionist legislation by developing a positive account of liberty and of the state, might be seen as a precursor of the postliberal adaptation of classical liberalism. Yet events since the financial crash of 2008 and the global pandemic of 2020 have served severely to dent confidence in any prospect of a liberal 'end of history' and to intensify debate about alternative projections.

Even before the pandemic, there were insistent reports of the death of liberalism, or at least of the neoliberal form it has taken since 1979. The financial crash of 2008 represented a serious jolt to established assumptions about liberalism's inevitable hegemony at the endpoint of history. The rising tide since then of populist and nationalist government in western states, has reinforced the suspicion that the neoliberal era of globalization has run its course and that liberal ideology itself is insufficient to meet the challenges of the moment. The vultures of political commentary have gathered to pick the bones of liberalism, on both the left and right, seeking to work out which parts of its legacy are retrievable for a postliberal future. Whether Blue Labour or Red Tory, communitarian, neo-conservative, civic-republican, rooted-cosmopolitan or agonistic-liberal, the hyphenated politics of paradox has emerged as a new way of thinking the previously unthinkable and of forging unlikely alliances.

The common good as trumps

In his book *Postliberal Politics: The Coming Era of Renewal* (Pabst, 2021), political theorist Adrian Pabst, drawing upon, while also enlarging, earlier communitarian critiques of liberalism, outlines a broad coalition of postliberal ideas that is not anti-liberal, but which nevertheless draws on traditions of political thought, including philosophical Idealism, political pluralism and civic humanism, that have rarely achieved dominance in classical liberalism. Careful to avoid 'crude forms of solidarity based on ethnic or religious homogeneity' and eager instead to embrace 'the pluralist heritage of ethical traditions forged in the nineteenth and twentieth centuries', Pabst seeks to reinstate alternative visions from those taken for granted by classical liberalism (Pabst, 2019: 3–5).

On this account, the chief characteristics of classical liberalism that postliberalism must seek to circumvent are its individualism, its prioritization of negative liberty, its dissociation of individual rights from mutual obligation, its erosion of intermediary institutions by the twin powers of free market and centralized state, and its association with a seemingly permanent condition of global disorder characterized by various forms of coercion, trade deficit and war. By contrast, postliberalism emphasizes the belief that human beings are relational, and that positive liberty entails a balance between autonomy and self-restraint. That balance in turn depends upon active state intervention to create conditions in which human capability can flourish. While respectful of rights, postliberalism of this sort does not seek to elevate individual libertarian rights to a position of supreme value, to make rights 'trumps', but instead privileges the common good as the dominant consideration. In celebrating the common good, postliberalism acknowledges that rights can only be meaningful when in company with reciprocal duties, and asserts that most people, most of the time, belong to more than one community, their plural, modern identities shaped inevitably by much more than their given community of birth. Anxious to avoid idolatrous worship of either centralized state or free market, postliberalism aims to reinstate strong civic institutions and structures of self-governance, nurturing intermediary institutions such as trade unions, universities, local authorities, professional associations, faith communities and even pubs, post offices and libraries. On the world stage, it eschews nationalism, instead preferring transnational cooperation to competition, fostering strong social and cultural ties, and promoting fair trade and military restraint (Pabst, 2021).

Central also to the postliberal vision is the dignity of labour, the value of work, in recognition that as far as possible citizenship entails active production rather than merely passive consumption (Boyle, 1997; Cruddas, 2021). Such an emphasis reflects postliberalism's provenance in the socialist humanism of William Morris, John Ruskin, G.D.H. Cole and R.H. Tawney, and its recognition of similar strands of thought in the US Democratic aspirations for the 'Great Society' of Lyndon Johnson and especially Robert Kennedy (Sandel, 2005: 63–6; Cruddas, 2021: 130–1). Such a vision seeks to rebalance any over-emphasis on consumerism and 'consumer rights' with concern for the situation of workers and for their reasonable expectation of fulfilment, creative contribution and active participation in the organization of their working lives (Cruddas, 2021).

'Light community' and 'thin culture'

To achieve practical realization, postliberalism roots itself in a public philosophy that is sceptical of the liberal law-state and embraces the return of politics as 'the conciliation of estranged interests through the pursuit of the common good' (Pabst, 2019: 5). Instead of starting from abstract theory, it takes its bearings from, but is not exclusively confined to, the things that most people value already, including friendship, locality and community. It does so, however, while mindful of the danger of retreating into a form of 'polis nostalgia': to identify community with 'thick cultural coherence' in a spirit of yearning for lost social homogeneity can too readily lead to a defensive advocacy of authoritarian government as an instrument of an imposed common culture. Escape from the rule of judges can then easily become a vehicle for a constitutional form that is supportive of strong and, if necessary, oppressive executive bureaucracy.

This 'authoritative rule for the common good' can also give rise in turn to a putative 'common good constitutionalism' (Vermeule, 2022) that is very different from a pluralist form of postliberalism. In the US context, for example, this is a style of constitutionalism that favours a 'powerful presidency ruling over a powerful bureaucracy … as the strong hand of legislative rule' (Vermeule, 2020: 11). The state can accordingly, and unreservedly, be trusted to protect the people from market forces, unscrupulous employers and corporations, from pandemics, disease and environmental disaster.

A pluralist and more inclusive form of postliberalism by contrast accepts that, under conditions of modernity, of pluralism and of diversity, sustainable community can be achieved only in a context of 'thin' cultural ties maintained by effective social 'bridges' rather than the homogenizing social 'bonds' of the pre-modern past or the modern private realm. Indeed, it takes encouragement from the recognition that even in the pre-modern past, and notably in ancient Athens, notwithstanding its patent exclusivities on grounds of gender and status, the pre-eminent democratic polis of the ancient world, the ties that sustained the democratic polity and its abiding practice of simply 'going on together' were, according to contemporary scholarship, precisely those of inclusive 'bridging' rather than 'bonding', and achieved in the context of a culture that, although coherent and created in common, was notably 'thin' (Ober, 2005: 69–91). In a reawakened democracy of participatory citizenship, 'the common good is defined by people themselves, acting in common, working through those relationships of co-operation and mutuality that are the foundation of healthy communities and a functioning civil society' (Restakis, 2022: 154).

Ezio Manzini in his book *Politics of the Everyday* (Manzini, 2019) offers vivid illustration of the sort of 'light community' that underpins the 'thin culture' to which pluralist postliberalism aspires. Recalling a social gathering in the Italian village where he lives, he reflects on the complex network of relationships which brought people together there, as they interweave with each other to produce a 'denser fabric of people, places and things', a form of complex social space. Some had lived there for generations; some had chosen to move there more recently; and some were the 'new nomads' comprising tourists, travellers and migrants. The result is a form of genuine community but one that is different from past forms in that it has not been handed down as a given: 'This is a community that exists by choice, one that has been consciously or unconsciously designed and built' (Manzini, 2019: 2). What Manzini means by community in this context is something 'voluntary, light, open', in which 'the individuality of each member is balanced with the desire to do something together' (Manzini, 2019: 2). At the heart of such common enterprise is a community that can best be imagined as a 'mesh of interweaving conversations', whose character is determined by 'the types of conversations taking place within it' (Manzini, 2019: 19).

Civilizing the 'partnership state': co-production and 'relational public services'

Communities of the sort envisaged by pluralist postliberalism are hardly susceptible to control by conventional legal forms. Moreover, the role of the state in working alongside such communities might typically be described as one of 'partnership' rather than of oppressive antagonism. In his book *Civilizing the State: Reclaiming Politics for the Common Good* (Restakis, 2022), John Restakis draws upon his experience with the cooperative movement in Canada and on examples of mutualism, 'deep democracy', urban commons and social cooperation in Europe (Bologna, Barcelona), India (Kerala, Chennai), the Middle East and Latin America, where the example of participatory budgeting in the city of Porte Alegre has since the 1990s served as an example of the challenges and possibilities attending new forms of active citizenship (Baiocchi, 2003). In developments of this sort, he detects a powerful vision that challenges the primacy of both the state and the market. Through a process of democratization and civil society empowerment, existing political institutions and economic relations are being recast as a form of 'civil economy' rather than orthodox 'political economy'.

Taking social care as an example, Restakis restates the importance of relational goods, embedded in actual relationships between people. Whereas in the liberal welfare state human connection has largely been eclipsed by the anonymous corporate administration of benefits to recipients who are perceived as passive and powerless, the partnership state, instead of treating social care as a commodity, seeks its re-humanization by placing social and interpersonal relationships at its centre. Moreover, this is a partnership or 'relational' model that seeks to engage citizens in democratic practices of co-production and cooperation alongside the state, rather than as its dependant, still less its antagonist (Restakis, 2022).

In a similar vein, social commentators in Britain have advocated a form of reawakened and more participatory democratic citizenship that entails a shift from 'transactional public services' to 'relational public services' built on collaboration between citizens and state, and on social networks rather than individuals, with the aim of 'growing capabilities' and developing co-productive 'asset-based practice' rather than simply 'managing needs' (Bentley, 2005; Buddery et al, 2016; Cottam, 2018; Routledge, 2020; Mackenzie, 2021). The pandemic has yielded similar templates for 'everyday democracy', from dialogue-oriented participation of citizens in rural Austria to the reclamation of community space in downtown San Diego (Taylor et al, 2020), from community land trusts in Newham to the experiments in community wealth-building inaugurated by the Preston Model (Brown and Jones, 2021; Hall et al, 2021). In all these examples, the recurrent themes are those of deliberative and participatory practices, co-production between citizens and state, and focus on local social networks rather than on atomized individuals or on the all-powerful state or market as the essential building blocks of sustainable community.

Recovering the lost threads of liberalism

In evoking a postliberal future, it is salutary to establish a theoretical foundation by recalling four alternative visions, which, although closely related to classical liberalism, have rarely achieved intellectual or practical supremacy. All four represent significant diversions from its central tenets, in each instance finding for law a less formal, procedural and rationalistic role.

Philosophical Idealism

The first emerges from a distinctively British form of liberal political thought in which philosophical Idealism has a foundational part. Drawing on Aristotle and Hegel, British philosophical Idealism, associated especially with T.H. Green, F.H. Bradley, Bernard Bosanquet and the early work of Ernest Barker, constituted a notable late-Victorian and Edwardian critique of 19th-century individualism, with significant priority being granted to a positive political conception of liberty and an understanding of rights that is explicitly social and rooted in the idea of the common good (Richter, 1964). Within such a tradition, the state is valued as central to moral development, which in turn finds expression in the primacy of community, social value and shared meaning. It is a vision that represents an antidote to Diceyan individualism and to the mentality to which Diceyan values have contributed so forcefully. It lies moreover at the source of a style of thinking about public law that is rooted in the jurisprudential soil of legal realism, and which crucially acknowledges the role of law as a positive one of enabling the state to contribute to the public good rather than a negative one of clipping the state's wings (Loughlin, 1992).

Central to Idealism's appeal was the belief that the state had responsibility for creating the social conditions in which individuals could flourish, achieve their full potential, and so enjoy a significant measure of positive liberty. As Green wrote, the function of the state was to create a social environment in which citizens would be instilled with 'the growth of self-reliance ... and moral dignity – in short, with the moral autonomy which is the condition of the highest goodness' (Green, 1895: 39–40; Stapleton, 1994: 29–30). The state's duties would to that extent reach beyond those of protecting private property and personal security traditionally ascribed to it by English political thought, encompassing instead such projects as land reform, compulsory elementary education and restrictions on freedom of contract in employment. The state did not, however, 'negate' but rather 'embraced' other associations (Barker, 1906: 232, 228; Stapleton, 1994: 47). From that embrace emerged the need for a 'mediating authority' to create a bridge between state and society, such a bridge comprising the law and its institutions, through which the state exercised its authority, and as the instrument of the common good (Stapleton, 1994: 47–9). In this way, modern law was perceived as being able to outstrip an older conception of law by being responsive to changing social circumstance and supporting progressive development.

Political pluralism

The second intellectual tradition is that of English political pluralism, originally associated with legal historian F.W. Maitland, his pupil J.N. Figgis, and Harold Laski, and later taken up in a rather different vein by the guild socialists, notably G.D.H. Cole. Drawing on Maitland's celebration of the legal device of 'the trust', political pluralism expressed its reticence about the centralized state by drawing attention to the prior existence of a multiplicity of intermediate associations and groups, including civic institutions, professional associations, trade unions and faith groups. Such institutions were not to be seen as dependent on the state for their existence but as a set of voluntary intermediary institutions that shape citizen identity in a network of overlapping commitments. 'Society' on this account is revealed as a 'nested' series of societies, a *communitas communitarum*, in which local engagement forms an alternative to the centralized state of Fabian 'gas and water' socialism and its preoccupation with centralized control, efficiency and expenditure (Barker, 1978: 94–8).

Guild socialists like Cole, whose early views owed much to Oxford philosophy and the anarchism of Morris, did not, however, anticipate the complete withering away of the state, but instead envisaged the growth of the power of labour and production alongside sustained overall responsibility still residing in the state: 'No doubt the ultimate power must reside in the democratic State; but it does not follow that the State should do all the work' (Cole, 1913: 28; Barker, 1978: 101). Guild socialism as a form of political pluralism, far from representing the complete rejection of the modern state, offered an 'intermediary position for those who wished to accept that state and get on with their business within its confines and in terms of its responsibilities' (Barker, 1978: 101). Meanwhile, Laski, much influenced by French jurist and advocate of decentralization Léon Duguit, as well as by Figgis and Maitland, and reasserting the importance of the civic associational element of the political-pluralist equation, could observe in the *Harvard Law Review* in 1917, 'Ours is a time of deep question about the state. Theories of corporate personality have challenged in decisive fashion its proud claim to pre-eminence ... the groups it has claimed to control seem, often enough, to lead a life no less full and splendid than its own' (Burrow, 2000: 123).

Civic humanism

The third intellectual tradition is that of civic humanism. Among the many strands and connotations of 'humanism' is a consistent cluster of meanings that bear upon the relationship of liberalism to 'humane' values, 'human rights' and 'human capability' (Nussbaum, 2011), the sense that human dignity resides in socially embedded personhood, experience and character.

Instead of technique, humanism reasserts the centrality of the human person and of human experience as the foundation of enquiry. It proposes the centrality of 'society' as the context of any such study and of the development of human value, resisting in equal measure both individualism and the worship of the state, while at the same time acknowledging 'reason' as its primary resource (Dodds, 1936). The freedom proposed by the classical humanist tradition is not freedom from all constraints and binding connection but rather the freedom that comes from holding many associations and identities simultaneously (Murray, 1990).

One especially salient, and resonant, aspect of the humanist tradition originates in a distinctive form of Renaissance political thought. Displacing Machiavelli from a position of dominance in the understanding of Renaissance political theory, a study by Renaissance historian James Hankins draws attention to a tradition of 'soul-craft and state-craft' in Renaissance Italy in which constitution-making is very much subordinate to the cultivation of character and of virtuous dispositions among those who have political power. By this form of character development (*paideia* or *institutio*), the humanist thinkers aimed to establish a form of 'virtue politics' through which political protagonists and state officials could address their fellow-citizens as equals, using lucid and accessible argument, and without taking refuge in 'legal mysteries understood only by specialists' (Hankins, 2019: 21).

Protesting against the gradual 'lawyerization' of western governments, the humanists distanced themselves from a legalistic perception of justice as 'morally empty positivism, the mere enforcement of rules', and instead advocated justice as a virtue dependent on 'deep and humane culture' and expressed in the virtuous exercise of discretion (Hankins, 2019: 503).

The 'rule of law' is no stranger to these humanistic accounts of political virtue. In the case of Renaissance humanism, it is 'the rule of law', however, interpreted according to the ancient Aristotelian conception of 'the rule of reason', rather than a modern notion of 'the rule of rules' or 'the rule of rights' (Shklar, 1987; Loughlin, 2000, 2018). According to that ancient conception, the rule of law is 'essentially a political idea' that requires those engaged in deliberative decision-making to exercise the virtue of *phronesis* (practical wisdom); and the 'single most important condition on which the rule of law rests is that of the worthiness of character of those engaged in legislative and judicial decision-making' (Loughlin, 2000: 70). It is this ancient conception of the rule of law that underpins the humanist approach to virtue politics and that puts at its centre not codes and constitutions, principles or regulations, but character and government by people rather than by rules.

Political pragmatism

The fourth intellectual tradition is that of pragmatism, which flourished in the US at about the same time as philosophical Idealism and political pluralism exercised influence in Britain. Indeed, it has been remarked of Laski's political theory, inflected by influences of Green's philosophical Idealism and Maitland's political pluralism, that it 'can in general be seen as the product of a pragmatic revolt in politics' (Loughlin, 1992: 171). Appealing to 'many who located themselves at the convergence between liberalism and socialism' (Loughlin, 1992: 126), pragmatism of the sort associated with C.S Peirce, William James and John Dewey is 'essentially a method of settling philosophical disputes by tracing their practical consequences' (Loughlin, 1992: 126). Pragmatism reinforces the view that experience is foundational to knowledge and that such experience is always relational rather than private and subjective. Rejecting a model of knowledge that places at a premium rational enquiry and abstract thought, pragmatism instead 'poses the analogy of the craftsman [sic] who is involved in making or doing, not by reference to some ideal model, but in accordance with the cumulative product of experience' (Loughlin, 1992: 128). For Dewey in particular, the implication of such an approach is that society must be viewed as 'organic' rather than atomistic, and democracy not as an abstract ideal but a practical way of life: 'A democracy is more than a form of government; it is primarily a mode of associated living, of conjoint communicated experience' (Dewey, 1976–88: 93). Central to the task of establishing such a democratic way of life are social institutions as a channel of civic education (Dewey, 1916).

The pragmatist tradition in the US, when applied to legal theory by those such as Roscoe Pound and Oliver Wendell Holmes, yielded during the inter-war years the 'legal realist' movement, with its suspicion of abstract reasoning and precedent, and its desire instead to place 'the human factor' at the centre of legal theory (Pound, 1908; Loughlin, 1992: 130). Against attempts to construct an autonomous theory of law, legal realists adopted a pragmatist approach that sought to place law in context and root it in the experimental methods of social science (Loughlin, 1992: 132).

None of these intellectual traditions, that of the British philosophical Idealists, the English political pluralists, the Renaissance civic humanists or the American political pragmatists, ultimately became dominant in liberal thought. Yet notwithstanding their failure to achieve pre-eminence, there remains within the visions they variously espouse the seeds of an alternative approach to questions about the state and the individual, and about the approach of those institutions which respond to citizen grievance and so 'hold to account' the agents of the state.

Postliberalism and responsive legality

Postliberal understandings and practices

Liberal legalism has been summarized, as noted earlier, from within the pragmatist tradition of legal realism as a set of basic understandings and practices. Simon (Simon, 2004) also articulates an alternative suite of basic understandings and practices that mirror but deviate from those ascribed to liberal legalism, and that offer a template for the construction of a postliberal approach that can be situated more broadly within the concept of Nonet and Selznick's 'responsive law'. First, instead of a victim perspective that assumes individual passivity, Simon proposes an alternative that will prioritize a citizen perspective in resistance to any sentimental or patronizing attitudes towards those labelled 'vulnerable' or 'victims'. Secondly, instead of populism, a postliberal approach will valorize associative democracy, embracing the complex social space afforded by a recognition of civic association and by shared, often overlapping, identities. It will not, however, discount the positive facilitative function of the ethical and partnership state in the context of promoting the common good and in achieving individual and shared human capability. Thirdly, instead of the priority of individual rights and the privileging of retrospective compensatory redress for their infringement, it will adopt the priority of solutions, aim for problem-solving practices and facilitate prospective and restorative remedies that enable citizens to keep going on together (Simon, 2004).

Its ways of proceeding, or its practices, will in turn be characterized first by citizen negotiation, which encourages deliberative, more democratic and inclusive forms of decision-making, albeit in the shadow of institutional scrutiny that induces and supports negotiation, gives formal underpinning to an achieved solution and assists in monitoring future performance of restorative remedy. Secondly, it will opt for rolling rule regimes which acknowledge the provisional and experimental quality of solutions and instead of a one-off trial valorize a continuing process of learning and responsibility. Thirdly, instead of bipartisan control of information and adversarial process it will prefer transparency as a means of enabling open access to information, inquisitorial decision-making and a mandate of influence and persuasion rather than one of sanction (Simon, 2004).

Responsive law

If, as previously proposed, liberal legalism can also be situated in a broader theoretical scheme as a manifestation of autonomous law, quite distinct from a closer identification with an authoritarian state as part of repressive law, a postliberal alternative of this sort will find a place as an aspect of responsive law. As part of the realist and sociological traditions of legal theory, responsive law adopts a more expansive view of legality than that capable of muster by either autonomous or repressive law (Nonet and Selznick, 2001: 74). Central to the project of responsive law is the elevation of purpose as an aspect of legal reasoning and with it a blurring of the edges distinguishing legal rationality from forms of rationality derived from other disciplines and social spheres. The elevation of purpose entails, in other words, the demotion of law's 'artificial reason' as one of its determinative features. Official retreat behind rules becomes less readily available as a means of evading responsibility. Restrictive focus on the case in hand, at the expense of patterns of practice and systemic consequences, loses credibility as the larger social context looms into view. The affirmation of legislative purpose, and of the overarching purpose of serving the 'welfare of society' and 'the common good', becomes instead the primary objective of responsive legality.

Alongside 'purpose' stands 'civility' as a distinguishing feature of responsive legality. This is not civility merely in the sense of good manners and common courtesy, although 'respect' for the dignity of the individual will be an integral feature of any humanistic form of postliberalism. Civility in this context will extend the humanistic impulse to affirm 'the central value of citizenship', so that 'respect' does indeed become the 'salient virtue', calling forth a 'spirit of moderation and openness' (Nonet and Selznick, 2001: 90). Moreover, civility looks beyond thick culture and social bonds to a more inclusive and pluralistic horizon where the 'parochialism of communal morality' is made subservient to an ethic of responsibility that is 'more urbane, more receptive to cultural diversity, less prone to brutalize the deviant and the eccentric' (Nonet and Selznick, 2001: 91). In the face of conflict, responsive legality favours an approach that is 'problem-centred and socially integrative', its remedies primarily restorative in aspiration rather than punitive, compensatory or vindictive. Such a perspective counters individualism with a pluralistic ethos that recognizes the social context of individuality and its group dynamic. It holds the arts of mediation, dialogue and compromise at a premium: '[I]n responsive law, order is negotiated not won by subordination' (Nonet and Selznick, 2001: 94).

Responsive legality disperses legal authority and enhances participation, not only in the sense of enabling 'access to justice' but in the 'demosprudential' aspiration of engaging citizens in the making and interpretation of law (Guinier, 2013; Guinier and Torres, 2014). In this way, 'legal participation takes on a political dimension', whereby 'legal action' or the formal expression of citizen grievance serves as a vehicle 'by which groups and organizations may participate in the determination of policy' rather than witness the presentation of a grievance as a way exclusively of 'vindicating individual claims based on recognized rules' or individual rights (Nonet and Selznick, 2001: 96). This exercise in the expansion of 'social advocacy' not only democratizes the process but opens access to more knowledge and expertise. The democratic task of going on together becomes a learning project, a dispersed, decentralized and cumulative process of collective problem-solving.

Responsive legality, unlike autonomous law or liberal legalism, will exercise an affirmative rather than critical authority, its concern positively to promote good policy and good administration while serving as a counter to exclusive focus on the task of adjudication and procedural propriety. For responsive legality, 'claims of right are understood as opportunities for uncovering disorder or malfunction ... the resolution of controversies cannot remain the paradigmatic concern ... Legal energies should be devoted to diagnosing institutional problems and redesigning institutional arrangements' (Nonet and Selznick, 2001: 106–7). This change of emphasis and priority does not entail the discounting of fair procedure or individual justice, but it does entail the expansion of remedy to include 'new modes of supervision, new ways of increasing the visibility of decisions, new organizational units, new structures of authority, new incentives' (Nonet and Selznick, 2001: 107). As Nonet and Selznick summarize the character of responsive law, while its 'master ideal' remains a form of 'legality', that 'ideal of legality should not be confused with the paraphernalia of "legalization" – the proliferation of rules and formalities' (Nonet and Selznick, 2001: 108). The abiding disposition of responsive legality is not retrospective adjudication but prospective regulation.

Postliberal imaginaries: *The Allegory of Good and Bad Government*

The iconography of judicial majesty and of principled authority was proposed earlier as an image of repressive law and autonomous law respectively, the latter resonant of contemporary liberal legalism's imposition of constraints on executive discretion in contrast to a more repressive form that identifies law with the coercive power of the state. To evoke an imaginary that expresses something of responsive law's postliberal qualities, it is instructive to call to mind a famous fresco in the Tuscan city of Siena.

An allegory of good government

Ambrogio Lorenzetti's *The Allegory of Good and Bad Government*, painted around 1340, adorns three walls of the Sala dei Nove in Siena's Palazzo Pubblico. The fresco, 'awash with figures and inscriptions', has at its centre a bearded male figure holding a sceptre and shield. This figure is often identified as the 'common good' or as an incarnation of 'the Nine', the group of citizens serving for short periods, on a rotating basis, on the ruling council of the Republic of Siena. Surrounding the central figure are various images including representations of the four cardinal virtues: Courage (Fortitude), Good Sense (Prudence), Moderation (Temperance) and Justice.

Lorenzetti's frescoes have attracted much debate among art historians and political theorists (Skinner, 1986). A widely accepted interpretation suggests that the regal figure represents the common good, a form of order imposed homogeneously on the citizenry. The message follows that the common good must be elevated to the position of ruler if good government is to be maintained. There is an element of ambiguity nevertheless that has attracted an alternative and inviting interpretation. Rather than the regal figure directly representing the common good, it has been argued that in fact it represents the city commune itself, a personification of the Sienese republic and its civic community, bound to the performance of justice but in the company of the other cardinal virtues. The message now proclaims the city republic itself and its citizens as the primary source of authority, a vehicle of self-governance: 'If Siena is to promote the common good, the supreme ruler and judge of Siena will have to be the Sienese themselves' (Skinner, 2003–4). In short, the citizens of Siena 'create ... a common good for themselves', and Lorenzetti's fresco should be read on this account as an image of the kind of inclusive and participatory government by means of which the common good can best be attained (Skinner, 2003–4).

Lorenzetti's celebrated *The Allegory of Good and Bad Government* can serve according to this interpretation as a provocative image of a postliberal politics, in which the figure of Justice, unlike later images, is not divorced from the common good or from the college of cardinal virtues of which she is just one. As Judith Resnik and Dennis Curtis have insisted, the later depictions of Justice in isolation, which have decorated court houses and town halls across the western world since the Enlightenment, unrealistically detach the process of fair or just adjudication from a more complex setting in which the other virtues must play a part in the service of the common good: in the familiar modern images of sword, scales and blindfold, the complexity of legality has mostly been 'washed out' (Resnik and Curtis, 2007: 160). Lorenzetti's imagery serves as a powerful reminder that law's putative autonomy diminishes the colour and vitality of justice as a complex social and political force, embedded in practices and precepts that cannot be contained within the 'artificial reason of the law'. On the contrary, if legality is to respond meaningfully to its true context, it must reconnect to a broader scheme of virtue as an 'interdependent collective' (Resnik and Curtis, 2011: 344) and to the common good, not as a homogeneous culture imposed on the citizenry from without but as a nexus of shared but potentially pluralistic value created by the citizenry itself from within. It is an image, in other words, that offers a postliberal and responsive alternative to Charoux's *The Judge*, to Orwell's 'hanging judge' of popular British sentiment, to McEwan's urbane and enlightened judicial protagonist in his novel *The Children Act*, and to the styles of repressive and autonomous legality that in their different ways those representations effectively evoke.

5

Citizen Grievance and the Spectre of Legalism

In the context of citizen grievance, the postliberal invocation of responsive legality is not without precedent in the literature of public administration, albeit expressed in rather different form. The interwar years in Britain were notably receptive to strains of political thought drawn from the traditions of philosophical Idealism, political pluralism, civic humanism and political pragmatism. In particular, those, such as William Robson and Laski, associated with the functionalist style of public law theory at the London School of Economics, drew on aspects of these traditions of thought in developing ideas about the relationship between citizen and state, and about the way in which the state should respond to citizen grievance. Despite the endurance of such approaches into the postwar period, their failure to take root, especially during the 1980s, became especially pronounced, as new forms of legalism and managerialism came to dominate an increasingly neoliberal discourse. In particular, the originally generous aspirations for administrative tribunals and public ombud institutions were attenuated, giving way to acquiescence in restricted forms of legality that defeated the more ambitious aspirations of earlier reformers. Responsive legality was not so much tried and found wanting, but rather not really tried.

Public administration and 'the welfare of society'

In the field of public administration, the shockwaves felt in Britain by the renewed stirrings of the interventionist state during the First World War accentuated the 'problem of bureaucracy' and elicited the startled reactions of those who feared in the 'new despotism' the emergence of a constitutional crisis. Dicey's advocacy of the rule of law and individual liberty represented a strong bulwark against the encroachments of collectivism and legislative innovation. Among those who undertook, from a very different perspective, to think through in some depth an alternative response was Robson, whose

Justice and Administrative Law (Robson, 1928) remains a foundational text of the 'functionalist' style of public law theory (Loughlin, 1992, 2005). In his insistence on the importance of the common good, the general welfare and the rule of reason, Robson is representative of sustained attempts to find in such concepts a rival to the dominant strain of legalism in liberal thought, especially in its encounter with public administration in practice.

Robson and the 'judicial mind'

Robson's book is notable for its emphasis on the need to challenge the primacy of individual rights, to foster the common good and to achieve both those ends by devising forms of intervention in public administration quite separate from those of the ordinary law courts. His target was what he described as 'the rigid system of inflexible private rights, enforceable in the courts of law almost regardless of social consequences' and consolidated gradually over several centuries of common law development (Robson, 1928: 322). While acknowledging the demise of the 'omnicompetent sovereign state', Robson was also confident, somewhat prematurely, that 'the absolute validity and legal sovereignty of individual rights is also passing away' (Robson, 1928: 322). Instead, '[a]bsolute rights of property and contract, of individual activity and personal freedom, enforceable in the courts of law regardless of social needs, have given way to qualified rights conditional on the extent to which they are compatible with the common good', the common good moreover 'as interpreted by administrative authorities exercising judicial power' (Robson, 1928: 323). It was this exercise of 'judicial power' by those who were not lawyers, let alone common law judges, that had so excited the charge of extra-constitutionality and the fear of a new despotism melodramatically anticipated as 'trial by Whitehall'. Although scarcely acknowledged in the contemporary debate, it was a fear that exercised British minds consistently in India during the Raj, evoking competing conceptions of justice: critics of civil servants argued that they had a merely superficial legal education and lacked the necessary practical experience of work in the courts of Bombay, Madras and Calcutta; their defenders, including governors general and viceroys, meanwhile argued that the best preparation for judicial office lay precisely in administrative work down on the plains (Cocks, 2014).

No such fears inhibited Robson's enthusiasm for non-lawyer participation in decision-making. In his view, the new administrative tribunals were able to achieve results unavailable to the wholly inflexible common law courts, results moreover that were 'socially desirable' and favourable in comparison with 'the sectional individual claims based on absolute legal rights to which the formal courts are so compelled to lend ear' (Robson, 1928: 324). In this way, the administrative tribunals were not only beginning to meet an urgent social need but discharging the function proper to all law, namely the promotion of 'the welfare of society' (Robson, 1928: 325). By giving expression to a more refined 'sense of justice' than the formal courts, the administrative tribunals were seen as advancing a general political climate in which 'social justice will become increasingly prominent' (Robson, 1928: 327).

It is striking that Robson's prescription for reform is concerned not simply with institutional change but with 'certain psychological considerations ... certain inherent qualities', which he associates with 'the judicial mind'. For Robson, the judicial mind is most clearly identified by its 'sense of fairness', its resistance of 'caprice or personal favour or self-interest', its striving for 'consistency, equality, and certainty', the 'exclusion of imponderables' and, critically, its exercise of 'judicial discretion' and the 'technique of impartial thought' (Robson, 1928: 185–248). Significantly, at the heart of Robson's notion of the judicial mind is a version of the rule of law as the 'rule of reason', a manifestation of the ancient conception of the rule of law rather than of a more modern interpretation of it as the rule of rules or of rights.

What is distinctive and, to Robson's contemporaries, controversial, is his considered view that the qualities of the 'judicial mind' are not the sole preserve of lawyers. Instead, Robson considered that these qualities of 'judicial mind' are available to anyone who is prepared to develop the necessary discipline of character and intellect. It made perfect sense, therefore, to expect such qualities to be apparent in administrative decision-making without recourse to explicitly legal participation or oversight. Enjoying 'greater flexibility and freedom from the ancient categories of the law', public officials were at liberty to a greater extent than the courts to 'give weight to the testimony of imponderable elements in human nature which are unrecognised by the "artificial reason" of the law and unknown to its categories' (Robson, 1928: 227).

Robson's notion of the judicial mind should not be taken either to exclude non-cognitive factors in decision-making. His concept of 'mind' is not exclusively rationalistic but inclusively affective too. The 'good judge' should not be confused with a 'mere logical machine' or an 'intellectual abstraction'. On the contrary, Robson, writing in a period in which Freudian psychology and the political psychology advanced by social theorist Graham Wallas were gaining influence, was anxious to acknowledge the importance of 'unconscious and sub-conscious elements' in the decision-making process, and at the same time to recognize the moral agency of administrators. As Robson trenchantly observed, 'ethical considerations cannot be excluded from the administration of justice any more than from any other department of government' (Robson, 1928: 238). With insight that foreshadows the contemporary realist recognition that 'the state is what its agents do', Robson concluded that 'public policy is nothing more or less than the experience of certain social sympathies and antagonisms of the judges' (Robson, 1928: 240). Broadening that category of 'judges' to include those non-lawyers capable of exercising the judicial mind was an important means of making more democratic the creation and implementation of public policy.

Alfred Zimmern: international relations and the 'substitute religion' of law

Wallas is reported once to have observed that while the Webbs in their Fabianism were interested in town councils, he was personally more interested in town councillors (Wiener, 1971: 59). People rather than institutions were his focus of study. The person to whom that observation was made was Alfred (later Sir Alfred) Zimmern, a former pupil and 'one of those men whose ideas, with all their idiosyncrasies, can provide a way into guiding assumptions of an era' (Mazower, 2009: 68). Zimmern, in debt to Wallas for much of his early intellectual development, played a significant role in establishing the League of Nations and in creating the study of international affairs as an academic discipline. In both capacities, he resisted what he saw as a lamentable drift towards legalism in the construction of the postwar international order, preferring a model of governance in which the rule of law was set in democratic context by the vehicle of 'the commonwealth'. The commonwealth in turn was a concept he had developed at some length in his work on ancient Greek society, where with Hellenist idealism he had construed the ancient Athenian empire as a benign form of federal cooperation (Zimmern, 1911).

Writing in 1930 in the first edition of the *Political Quarterly*, edited by Robson and Leonard Woolf, Zimmern advocated a form of civic education as a means of ensuring that 'actual participation in the conduct of affairs and the framing of policies' was brought within the 'reach of the common man' (Zimmern, 1930). By developing democratic participation in the small places of daily life, Zimmern anticipated the expansion of civic participation to embrace broader issues of public policy, albeit with the benefit of 'experts' as a means of 'sorting out the issues' for deliberation. As Zimmern put it: 'Citizens who have become accustomed to "sorting out the issues" and extinguishing their own bonfires in smaller concerns have acquired new standards of judgment for listening to arguments upon larger issues'; in this way, 'the voice of the circumference' can 'penetrate the centre', and vice versa (Zimmern, 1930: 21).

Zimmern's views on the place of law in the democratic polity are appropriately nuanced. They become clear in his observations on the ancient Greek Commonwealth, where he draws attention to the ancient respect for 'the laws', as opposed to the abstract or reified notion of 'the law' worshipped by modern society. The laws, not the law, were engraved on the hearts of ancient Athenian citizens, suggests Zimmern, because there was no such thing as 'the Government', as distinct from 'the People' (Zimmern, 1911: 129). By contrast, in modern western societies the laws, more likely abstracted as 'the law', are 'remote from daily life' because the people do not play an active part in their creation or implementation, such tasks being entrusted to the care of 'representatives and experts and their agents'. In a democratic polity in which genuine self-government is realized, citizens become willingly conformed to the laws as their instructor, precisely because they recognize such laws as their own and as the product of reason, to whose creation and implementation they have actively contributed.

The practical force of Zimmern's views, expressed in this way in 1911, becomes apparent in his published reflections, in 1936, entitled *The League of Nations and the Rule of Law* (Zimmern, 1936). By then, Zimmern had between 1926 and 1930 served as deputy director of the League of Nations' Institute of Intellectual Cooperation (the forerunner of UNESCO). In supporting the 'rule of law' as the basis of international cooperation, Zimmern was careful to distance himself from the strictures of 'the legalists', who would import into world affairs an approach to law that set it apart from any actual pattern of 'social habit' or living practice. For Zimmern, the law should be seen more like a tree than a tablet of stone, something vital and living, responsive to social change.

By contrast, Zimmern discovered in the notion of 'international law' as promulgated by legalist thought something notably remote from both the hearts and minds of the people, who do not find its abstraction embodied in the habits of any existing society. Such laws will, in other words, be found not on the street but 'enshrined' in libraries, divorced from any actual social forms, the treaties in which they are defined amounting to little more than 'a collection of rules' (Zimmern, 1936: 94–8). As a result, Zimmern characterizes legalism as a form of superstition, a 'substitute-religion' in 'legal trappings – the adoration of the wig and gown'; such idolatry takes 'the good' of the laws and elevates it, without due moderation, to the supreme good, making of legalism an unreflective creed incapable of doctrinal development (Zimmern, 1936: 100).

This intellectual tradition of broadly humanist reflection on law, citizenship and administration, represented in their different but overlapping ways by Robson, Wallas and Zimmern, is now largely obscured from view. Yet its positive appraisal of the role of the state and its capacity to promote the common good and positive human capabilities; the high value attached to civic education, citizenship and political participation mediated by civic association 'on the ground'; and its insistence on exploring the social and psychological conditions that can foster a genuinely participatory form of democratic citizenship: these emphases may fruitfully serve to counterbalance undue deference to legal categories of thought and the legalism of which such categories are a part. This is an intellectual tradition that takes its origins from markedly humanistic soil, from the overarching belief that soul-craft precedes statecraft and that the democratic soul rather than the judicial mind, albeit extended in its scope beyond a professional legal caste, is the prize of supreme value in the democratic practice of simply going on together in the face of circumstances that are often tragic and rarely other than daunting (O'Brien, 2021). It is an intellectual tradition that also brings together strands of philosophical Idealism and political pluralism, and that resonates with aspects of American legal realism: 'The functionalist public lawyers of the inter-war years were our equivalent of the American legal realists' (Loughlin, 1992: 173).

Tribunals and the 'dead hand of Dicey'
A 'rival technique' for a 'new mode of adjudication'

Notwithstanding the encroachment of the functionalist style, the status of tribunals in Britain has since the 19th century been established against the larger background of a native scepticism about administrative discretion and an interpretation of the rule of law that valorizes judge-made law and the courts at the expense of all other forms of adjudication, mediation and political intervention. Robson, in his ground-breaking work to establish the intellectual credibility of a separate sphere of administrative law, still retained an attachment to the judicial mind as the template of respectable decision-making. His primary challenge to the dominant view was to suggest that the judicial mind could be subjected to a process of democratization, that the habits of mind and character associated with judicial discretion could be extended to those without legal training or judicial office. Such extension would recognize both the propriety of administrative decision-making by public officials and of non-judicial tribunals, populated by non-lawyers and shaped by practices other than those enshrined in the ethos of the common law courts.

Four years after the publication of *Justice and Administrative Law*, and after he had given evidence in March 1930 to the Committee on Ministers' Powers chaired by Lord Donoughmore, Robson turned in 1932 to the newly established vehicle of the *Political Quarterly* to express his regret at the conclusions drawn by the Committee in its report. In his view, the Donoughmore Committee had been doomed from the start, brought to birth 'with the dead hand of Dicey lying frozen on its neck' (Robson, 1932: 116). Although the Donoughmore Committee had found its way to supporting a 'quasi-judicial' role for administrative tribunals, it had failed to acknowledge the more fundamental need for a 'mode of adjudication' in which the practising lawyer has little part. This alternative mode of adjudication would operate with a 'rival technique' and a new jurisdiction 'outstripping the waning popularity of the established courts' (Robson, 1932: 115). These 'new organs of adjudication' would in effect repair the 'defects of the courts of justice as instruments for controlling, wisely and effectively, the relations between the citizen and the state' by working more quickly than the courts, by bringing to the task substantive experience of (and expertise in) public administration, and by demonstrating 'fewer prejudices against government ... greater heed to the social interests involved ... and less solicitude for private property rights' (Robson, 1932: 122–3). Far from seeking to constrain government and clip its wings, the approach of such newly constituted tribunals would be purposive, shaped by 'a conscious effort at furthering the social policy embodied in the legislation' (Robson, 1932: 123).

Falling well short of this ambitious vision for a new system of administrative law, Donoughmore had merely supplemented the existing 'patchwork quilt' with a smattering of legalistic protection for citizens in the form of some basic 'rules of natural justice' – the ability to state a case, receive reasons for a decision, enjoy shared access to documentary evidence and draw upon published summaries of leading decisions. There was nothing in Donoughmore, however, on the 'structure of the system', and oversight was to be provided by an appellate system of checks and balances that would remain in the hands of a 'hostile judiciary' (Robson, 1932: 123–4). As a result, the executive would have the opportunity to enter an unholy alliance with the judiciary, using the courts as a 'weapon of the most tyrannous character'. Instead of subjecting government to scrutiny by way of processes that were democratic and participatory, Donoughmore had, on Robson's account, established 'for all eternity' an undemocratic process for perpetuating a notably narrow form of the rule of law and a restricted vision of individual freedom (Robson, 1932: 124).

The limitations of the Donoughmore Committee's prescriptions were set to be entrenched by subsequent official reflection on the role of tribunals. There emerged in later decades an increasingly consolidated view of administrative justice as comprising two top tiers in the form of courts and tribunals, and two inferior tiers in the form of departmental first-instance decision-making and internal departmental review. This was a model that directed lawyerly attention to just the two top tiers, so long as tribunals were perceived primarily as 'court substitutes' (Harlow and Rawlings, 2009: 442) rather than as vehicles of informal justice, or of what became known by the 1960s as forms of 'alternative dispute resolution' (ADR). Although others followed in Robson's critical footsteps, there was little sign of a more generalized thaw in Dicey's posthumous and icy grip on the prevailing mentality.

The judicialization of tribunals

The judicialization of tribunals in Britain received further reinforcement from the report of the Franks Committee in 1958 (Drewry, 2009; Harlow and Rawlings, 2009). Franks in effect consolidated the role of tribunals as 'machinery for adjudication', with increased scope for legal advice and representation, legal aid, oversight by the High Court and incorporation within the remit of the Lord Chancellor's Department. Any potential links between tribunals and informal justice were effectively severed, while public inquiries, although recognized as a hybrid form between administrative and judicial functions, nevertheless came to resemble tribunals, and thereby courts, in both practice and procedure. This resemblance was made more amenable to general assent by commentary that took planning inquiries as typical, when in fact their heavily weighted procedures meant they were far from it. Underlying Franks' prescription for reform was a persistent individualism, with the emphasis on legal adjudication reflecting an exclusive focus on individual cases, at the expense of any broader perception of the common good or public welfare as an essential feature of democratic administration. As Carol Harlow and Richard Rawlings remark, 'With Franks, the judicialization that Robson feared was well under way', and for the next 20 years or more tribunals largely acquired a 'court substitute function' before 'finally it came to be accepted that they were "a third tier in the administration of civil justice"' (Harlow and Rawlings, 2009: 442).

This process of judicialization achieved its apotheosis over half a century later with the Tribunals, Courts and Enforcement Act 2007 (Drewry, 2009: 47). The 'court substitute' function that had evolved in the second half of the 20th century led to the absorption of tribunals as an integral component of the larger civil justice system. Responsibility for their management now passed to a newly constituted Courts and Tribunals Service, combining courts and tribunals in a single administrative unit. Tribunal chairs became tribunal judges, and rights of appeal were directed to a new Upper Tribunal, with a formally acknowledged appellate function (Drewry, 2009: 55). Although non-legal members of tribunal panels were retained, their role was questioned and attenuated, with judges in some tribunal chambers sitting with just a single lay member, albeit with increased emphasis on the 'specialist' rather than the 'lay' aspect of that member's contribution. The overall direction, in combination with that of judicialization, was as a result towards increased professionalization rather than democratic participation. The Woolf Report (Woolf, 1996), with its promotion of ADR as a concession to consumer interests, and the Leggatt Report (Leggatt, 2001), with its emphasis on 'tribunals for users', in effect, and somewhat ironically, dovetailed with the advanced stages of judicialization. Reformist ambitions rested largely on procedural hygiene and transparency, on the importance of tribunals establishing legal precedent and affording opportunities for appeal to a higher legal authority, and on 'access to justice' conceived restrictively as access to a court-like forum, even if designated as 'alternative'. Although tribunals remained 'inquisitorial' in theory, in practice the process of judicialization pushed them closer than ever to emulation of the court-type model, with the adversarial trial the largely unchallenged paradigm of 'best practice', the oral hearing of evidence and argument the benchmark for fair procedure. The advent of the Human Rights Act 1998, and its incorporation of Article 6 of the European Convention on Human Rights (the so-called 'human rights for lawyers' article), has served in this context to accentuate the insistence that an oral hearing is the ideal means of safeguarding the rule of law in responding to citizen grievance (Harlow and Rawlings, 2009: 617). While tribunals for the most part certainly exhibit less legalistic tendencies than the higher courts, the reforms of this century, welcomed by some, with distinguished judicial support, as an antidote to perceived amateurism, inconsistency and government influence, have, as Gavin Drewry observes, carried forward 'an evolutionary tendency to systematise and judicialise the structure and working of tribunals' (Drewry, 2009: 57).

The interwar ambitions of commentators like Robson, Wallas and Zimmern to that extent foundered in later decades on the 'pathological legalism' articulated at a theoretical level by Shklar in the 1960s and identified in practice by Titmuss in the 1970s. The source of that pathology was a mentality comprising distinct preferences: for the evaluation of law as an autonomous social form, notably superior to politics as a means of achieving social coherence; for the state as a force that must be kept under surveillance and in check by the law; for the acceptance that the best way of achieving that measure of surveillance is by rule-based adjudication in court-like institutions; and for the belief that the overarching purpose of intervention is the protection of individual rights and entitlements.

For those who advocated a more responsive, and indeed functionalist, approach, the construction of an alternative vision rested on contrasting foundational beliefs: that law is just one among many aspects of social discourse, firmly rooted in its broader social context, far from autonomous and certainly not superior to politics or public administration as a means of social ordering in a democracy; that the state and public administration are not just necessary evils to be limited and controlled as far as possible, but positive goods, to be enriched, enhanced and enabled; that the primary purpose of intervention is not to clip the wings of the state, exercise surveillance or control but to encourage and develop good practices in public agencies and virtuous dispositions in the street-level bureaucrats who populate them; that the best way of achieving that purpose is not through rule-based adjudication, which is likely to have the opposite effect; and that the overall objective should be the promotion of the common good, with the administrative state, both ethical and enabling, an essential and privileged vehicle for achieving that ambition. In the development of the tribunal system in Britain, the former mentality had, however, largely triumphed.

The 'Ombudsman': 'a more subtle brand of legalistic thinking'

A 'cult of bureaucratic humanity'

Running parallel with the development of the tribunal system in the postwar period has been a movement for informal justice and ADR that has nevertheless to some extent adopted aspects of that former, very different, approach. Notable among the institutional manifestations of that movement has been that of the 'ombud' (a designation preferable to the gendered title 'Ombudsman' [Bondy and Doyle, 2018]), which has since the second half of the 20th century become an 'enterprise' that has taken root in both public and private sectors across the globe (Buck et al, 2011; Hertogh and Kirkham, 2018; Groves and Stuhmcke, 2022). By the late 1950s, it had already become increasingly fashionable on both the political right and left to consider that postwar conditions provided an occasion for the introduction of the ombud in Britain. In 1962, New Zealand became the first Commonwealth nation to establish a national ombud. Until then, the institution had been confined to Scandinavia: Sweden since 1809, Finland since 1919, Denmark since 1955, followed by Norway in 1962. It was the example of Denmark that proved especially influential in Britain. The first Danish ombud, Stephan Hurwitz, was interviewed for *The Listener* in 1960. In conversation with leading academic public lawyers, Griffith and H.W.R. Wade, Hurwitz spoke persuasively about the ombud as a "democratic institution", a "safety valve" for an old democracy, which would serve as a "bridge" between the law and the public administration. Offering an alternative to both law and administration that was "more ambiguous and amphibious" than either, the ombud would provide welcome medicine for the "diseases in the body politic" (Hurwitz, 1960).

This conception of the ombud as a bridging institution between state and individual was firmly rooted in the distinctively Danish, rather than the more legalistic Swedish, approach to enabling a common public project, in which good citizenship entails a sense of responsibility towards the state as an instrument of the common good, as well as recognition of the state's duties towards its citizens. The ombud was to that extent conceived as a channel of civic education, a means of casting light on those reciprocal duties, and of establishing a vehicle, quite different from the courts, for reinforcing practices conducive to democratic culture. The ombud institution served as a facilitator of the symbiotic relationship between state and individual, a collaborative means of responding to the grievances that citizens might have about the operational practices of the state. It was in other words a reflection of a consensual style of politics that was inherently cooperative and conciliatory.

Transplanted to British soil, the ombud was, however, quite quickly pruned to accommodate a more adversarial role, in keeping with the indigenous political culture which, on both left and right in the postwar period, identified burgeoning state bureaucracy and 'red tape' as potential obstacles to the realization of ancient Anglo-Saxon freedoms. Far from the state being seen, even on the left, as a benign partner of empowered democratic citizens, it was instead portrayed as a potential threat to individual liberty. The advocacy of the ombud as potential saviour came not just from T.E. Utley and the Society for the Protection of Individual Freedom (Utley, 1961; Stapleton, 2014), but from Labour politicians and eventually the Labour Party itself, which adopted the ombud idea as a central part of its election manifesto in 1964 as a means of 'humanising the whole administration of the state' (Labour Party, 1964: 24; Gwyn, 1971). In a speech given at Stowmarket on 3 July 1964, future Labour Prime Minister Harold Wilson used similar language in proposing that the ombud would "humanize the administration" and "improve relations between Westminster on the one hand and the individual citizen" (Wilson, 1964, cited by Gwyn (1971: 401)). Any fears that Labour in power might inaugurate a socialist state leviathan could be vanquished in the knowledge that a Scandinavian-style ombud was waiting in the wings to see fair play and preserve individual liberty.

That humanizing aspiration attracted significant support. Andrew Shonfield, for example, in an influential study of the changing balance of public and private power in the 1960s, provided perhaps one of the most vivid evocations of how an ombud might contribute to what he described as a 'cult of bureaucratic humanity', a 'powerful supplement to administrative law' which would push modern public administration beyond 'mere justice' towards the 'recognition of a duty of active kindness in a society which grows increasingly dependent on the initiative and the sensibility of its public officials' (Shonfield, 1965: 427). Shonfield's positive estimation of the ombud reflected his equally dismissive assessment of the overwhelming emphasis otherwise afforded to legal procedure and its exclusive concern with 'judicial ritual' (Shonfield, 1965: 420). Such formalities, in Shonfield's view, amount to a 'ceremonial hoax' made 'the more obnoxious for the pretence of having something to do with human rights' (Shonfield, 1965: 419). The establishment of an ombud in Britain would represent a significant deviation from the customary but unsuccessful approach of 'trying to adjust the methods of a traditional legal philosophy to the realities of modern government' (Shonfield, 1965: 421) – an approach that justified the characterization of Britain in the 1960s as a 'would-be "nomocracy"' or 'law state' (Shonfield, 1965: 419).

'A constitutional and legal office'

The reception of the ombud in Britain occurred therefore in a political culture that was both inherently adversarial and 'nomocratic', in the sense of granting a measure of authority to a distinctive style of 'rule of law' legalism, in tension with more overtly 'democratic' alternatives. In 1961, the campaigning organization Justice commissioned a report from Sir John Whyatt, Chief Justice of Singapore, which did much to consolidate the eventual establishment of a national ombud for the UK in 1967 (Whyatt, 1961). Whyatt brought a 'lawyerly' perspective to an office that he envisaged as 'an administrative small claims court' (Harlow and Rawlings, 2009: 537). Once established, the office passed between 1979 and 1990 into the hands of successive lawyers, Sir Cecil Clothier and Sir Anthony Barraclough, who left a notably legalist mark on the ombud institution. The addition of the Health Service Commissioner function in 1973, with its 'inadequate service' and clinical-judgement remit, had already pushed the de facto joint office towards a more overtly judicial forum, with the concerns of the Medical Defence Union, the Patients Association and indeed the courts in the exercise of their judicial review function being especially influential. Although less legalistic no doubt than, for example, its German near-counterparts, the UK's national ombud is nevertheless perceived by the public as residing deeply within the shadow of the law, even to the extent that a predetermined legal consciousness largely shapes expectations (Creutzfeldt, 2018). As a result, on-line 'ombud-watchers' are likely to criticize the office for not being more judicial, for example by not achieving closure through enforceable decisions and remedies, not testing evidence more forensically through a more adversarial process, and not making more objectively compelling decisions by reference to fixed rules rather than vague principles.

A significant omission from the proposals in Britain was that of 'own-initiative powers', or the ability to investigate an issue known to the ombud to be noteworthy and in the public interest, even in the absence of a specific individual complaint. This power had been identified by Shonfield as one that in Scandinavia set the ombud apart from conventional courts and other judicial forums. Any such deviation from the adversarial paradigm was absent from Whyatt's recommendations and from the founding legislation when it eventually appeared as the Parliamentary Commissioner Act in 1967. It remained absent too from the remit of any public ombud in the UK until reforms in the 21st century extended the reach of the national ombud institutions in Northern Ireland and Wales (Kirkham and Gill, 2020).

The role of Justice in advancing the cause of the ombud in the UK is revealing of the legalistic context into which the ombud was quickly absorbed. It has been observed that it was 'the impetus given by Justice to the creation of a constitutional and legal office that helped give the office of Ombudsman just that character' (O'Hara, 2012: 100). Indeed, in the context of the political climate then prevalent, the very fact that 'most of Justice's luminaries were sympathetic to, or members of, the Liberal or Labour parties' actually reinforced their libertarian interest in the ombud as an antidote to increasing public fears about state bureaucracy in the 1960s (Gwyn, 1971;

O'Hara, 2011: 704). The international context in which Justice had been formed as the British section of the International Commission of Jurists (ICJ) in 1957 and against which its interest in the ombud institution emerged helps explain the pronounced legalistic ethos of the institution in the UK. The first spur to action had been the spectacle of political trials in Hungary and South Africa. Future Labour Lord Chancellor Gerald Gardiner had been dispatched, even before Justice was formally established, to observe treason trials in South Africa in December 1956. Meanwhile, Peter Benenson, future founder of Amnesty International but also an instrumental figure in the establishment of Justice, visited Hungary in the period after the rising against the Soviet occupation in 1956 to observe its aftermath. Gardiner, along with Sir Hartley Shawcross, one of the prosecutors at the Nuremberg Trials and the existing British representative at the ICJ, and another future Labour Lord Chancellor and Nuremberg advocate, Elwyn Jones, attended a meeting of the ICJ at The Hague in 1956. The ICJ's stated objective was 'to foster understanding of and respect for the Rule of Law'. On its formal establishment in 1957, Justice in turn had at the centre of its constitution the obligation to 'uphold and strengthen the principles of the Rule of Law in the territories for which the British Parliament is directly or indirectly responsible', to maintain the highest standards in the administration of justice and to guarantee 'the preservation of the fundamental liberties of the individual' (Stacey, 1971: 14–27).

This context of international law and libertarian values indicates the character of Justice's support for the ombud. Against the background of Justice's early resistance to state persecution in the Soviet bloc and apartheid South Africa, the valorization of individual liberty and of the rule of law as its chief means of protection can be seen to have expressed a strongly legalist ethos that, transposed to a very different mid-century Britain, found in the ombud merely a quasi-judicial footnote to the court structure rather than a new and non-judicial genre. Despite its significant Labour and Liberal Party credentials, in this regard Justice shared much common ground with the Society for Individual Freedom (originally the Society of Individualists) founded by Sir Ernest Benn in 1942, and for whom Utley wrote *Occasion for Ombudsman* in 1961. Conservative MP Dr Donald Johnson, whose involuntary detention in a psychiatric hospital in 1950 led to a personal interest in the ombud, was a member of both organizations. After his election to Parliament in 1955, and having heard a lecture by Hurwitz, Johnson put down a question to the Conservative Prime Minister Harold Macmillan about the ombud institution, which in turn led to Whitehall officials contacting Justice to learn more. Coinciding with Justice's commissioning of the Whyatt Report, Macmillan's written reply, endorsing the 'objective and serious study' of the ombud being undertaken by a 'group of lawyers', lent to Justice's involvement and Whyatt's report a measure of official status.

As a result, the non-legal institution of the ombud was in Britain from the outset shaped by a 'group of lawyers' whose commitment to individual liberty, and suspicion of the state bureaucracy, reinforced by libertarian elements in the main political parties, including, perhaps surprisingly, the Labour Party, helped establish what was in essence, as observed earlier, a 'constitutional and legal office' (Stacey, 1971: 14–27; O'Hara, 2011: 704).

An 'integral part of constitutional reality'

The apotheosis of the ombud as a 'constitutional and legal office' on the international stage, but with repercussions for local perception of the institution, has more recently been achieved with the promulgation of the 'Venice Principles on the Protection and Promotion of the Ombudsman Institution' (2019). The Venice Principles are the work of the Venice Commission, or the European Commission for Democracy through Law, which, since its creation in 1990 in the wake of the collapse of the Berlin Wall, has had as its mission the promotion of the three central principles of democracy, human rights and law. With a secretariat based in Strasbourg, the Commission's influence is not limited to Europe: its membership comprises not only the 46 member states of the Council of Europe, but 15 other nations, including Brazil, Chile, Israel, Canada and the US.

The individual membership of the Commission suggests its legalistic, and indeed constitutionalist, credentials, with university professors of public and international law, and supreme court and constitutional court judges, forming the dominant cohort. The creation of an 'enabling environment' for the fostering of the rule of law has been a significant part of the Commission's work, including a substantive report in 2011 complete with a 'rule of law checklist' (Venice Commission, 2011). As part of that 'enabling environment', the ombud has also attracted the Commission's attention, with reports of various kinds devoted to it since the publication of the first of these in 1991. Many of these reports have been concerned with the difficulties faced by ombuds in troubled corners of the globe, such as the former Yugoslavia in the 1990s. From this work has followed the distillation of inviolable principles of independence, transparency and fairness to serve as criteria against which identification of an authentic ombud institution can be validated.

The Venice Principles themselves accentuate the constitutional and legal character of the ombud and are the result of consultation with an array of international agencies, including the UN Human Rights Office of the High Commissioner, the Council of Europe Commissioner for Human Rights, the Organization for Security and Co-operation in Europe, Office for Democratic Institutions and Human Rights, the European Union Agency for Fundamental Rights, as well as the European Ombudsman, the International Ombudsman Institute (IOI), various regional ombud associations in Europe, and the European Network of National Human Rights Institutions. Adapted into the 'legal and political system' of more than 140 states, ombuds are, according to the Venice Principles, governed by core principles of independence, objectivity, transparency, fairness and impartiality; they represent an 'important element in a State based on democracy, the rule of law, the respect for human rights and fundamental freedoms', and moreover, on 'good administration'. The ombud's remit is that of 'taking action independently against maladministration and alleged violations of human rights and fundamental freedoms'; the 'right to complain' to an ombud is 'in addition to the right of access to justice through the courts', albeit with a discretionary power to commence 'own–initiative' investigations, to intervene before adjudicatory bodies and courts, and to challenge the constitutionality of laws and regulations, with 'functional immunity' from legal process in respect of their official work. The appropriate environment for the flourishing of the ombud is one conditioned by 'long-standing constitutional traditions and a mature constitutional and democratic political culture'. The ombud should be based 'on a firm legal foundation, preferably at constitutional level', and appointment or election should be in accordance with a prescribed process and set of criteria (Venice Commission, 2019).

The Venice Principles serve to consolidate an emerging vision of modern ombud practice that has already gained credence at national and international level, not least through the work of the IOI, currently based in Vienna, itself a significant force for modern constitutionalism and a legalistic notion of the rule of law (Carver, 2018). As the IOI emphasized in its 2012 'Wellington Declaration', the ombud is an 'integral part of constitutional reality' and makes an important contribution 'to implementing the rule of law, monitoring good public administration, protecting and promoting human rights and fighting corruption'. Although the ombud is an institution that is 'extraordinarily adaptable and innovative', it must remain 'true to its core principles of independence, impartiality and fairness and its main role of protecting people against violation of rights, abuse of power and maladministration' (International Ombudsman Institute, 2012), a role recognized by the UN in its Resolution on Ombudsmen and Mediator Institutions (United Nations, 2020). A comment of Bernard Crick, on the debate about the ombud in Britain in the 1960s, is to that extent prescient and apposite, not just in Britain but globally: 'The ombudsman's elevation as saviour represents a brand of legalistic thinking more subtle than the old common lawyer's legalism it attacked, but legalism none the less in its hope to turn political issues into matters for impartial adjudication' (Crick, 1965, reprinted in Ball, 2015: 101).

In the face of the trajectory taken in practice by tribunals and ombuds, the flickering ambitions of responsive law, discernible in the interwar years and once more in the postwar period, can be seen therefore to have foundered in the face of autonomous legality. The generous interwar aspirations of those like Robson and the postwar advocates of the ombud held out the prospect of consolidating tribunals as something generically different from courts and ombuds as affirmative contributors to a new democratic form of humane bureaucracy. Such aspirations represented a definite attempt to find alternatives to restrictively legalistic modes of practice in the face of citizen grievance. In their advocacy of responsive law *avant la lettre*, the proponents of such views sought a means of adapting to changing social circumstances and democratic ambition. Yet despite such initiatives, in the case of both administrative tribunals and ombuds there can be discerned recessive pressures which sapped energy and innovation, instead shaping ostensibly new institutions to the established template of court-like forums. Such recalcitrance was never entirely comprehensive, nor uniformly successful in eliminating all trace of responsive legality. Yet it was sufficiently entrenched to preserve the hegemony of autonomous law, and with its inherent tendency towards legalism, to serve as an instrument of reverse alchemy, turning the gilded prospect of responsive legality into something rather less glittering.

6

Postliberal Accountability: The Challenge of Disability Human Rights

Responsive legality, formally articulated in the US in the 1960s, largely failed to take root in the UK, despite the seeds of such an approach contained in the aspirations for tribunals between the World Wars, and for the ombud after the Second World War. More recently, administrative justice in England specifically, by contrast with the devolved administrations in Scotland, Wales and Northern Ireland, has at times been out of step with developments in other areas of substantive law which have implications for it and for the relationship between citizen and state. One significant area of innovation has been that of disability human rights, as part of a broader awakening of interest in the significance of disability as a social construct and as a litmus test more generally for inclusive citizenship. The advent of disability human rights as a 'new paradigm' in a legal context has been matched therefore by its reception as an aspect of human experience that must be reckoned with in any public philosophy that seeks to respond purposefully to contemporary society. The implications of disability human rights for the task of responding to citizen grievance in a postliberal context assume powerful illustrative force.

Disability human rights and social movement politics
'Teamwork at the heart of everything'

Bert (later Sir Bert) Massie was born into a large working-class family in Liverpool shortly after the Second World War. When he was three months old, doctors told his mother he had polio. At that moment, his personal life became inescapably entangled with the development of disability rights. Yet the language of disability rights was for much of Massie's life unavailable as an interpretative framework: as a child, he had no inkling that he was 'disabled' until somebody told him. Yet human diversity on the street where he grew up was inescapable: epilepsy, deafness, immobility, facial disfigurement and myriad other hidden impairments (Massie, 2019: 48–9).

The significance of social class and social disadvantage was not lost on him, nor the importance, and at times the ambiguous quality, of the emergent welfare state as a means of lifting people out of poverty: too often 'things done to you, not with you', and early social segregation at the Children's Rest School of Recovery in Liverpool. Group solidarity nevertheless prevailed, the collaboration with other disabled people, and indeed some non-disabled people, in the shared project of achieving civil and human rights an enduring source of consolation: 'Teamwork has been at the heart of everything' (Massie, 2019: ii).

State, community and personhood

By the time of his death, Massie had played a notable part in the campaign for disability rights in the UK. As former Labour minister Lord Blunkett has observed, Massie was a campaigner and social reformer of national prominence, holding influential posts as Chair of the Royal Association for Disability and Rehabilitation and subsequently as the first, and indeed only, Chair of the Disability Rights Commission (DRC), established by the UK Labour government in 1999 (Blunkett, 2019). His anecdotal recollections of childhood, before the accolades accumulated, is revealing of themes that became prominent in the development of the disability rights movement not only in the UK but elsewhere. First, there is the prevailing sense of impairment and disability as part of the human condition, pervasive and multifaceted, both particular and entirely general, the variations in 'vulnerability' and 'dependence' being matters of degree rather than kind. As Macintyre has put it, human beings are quite simply by their nature 'dependent rational animals', whose reliance on each other is universal and an inescapable part of human community (Macintyre, 1999). In Massie's observations on the positive features of the ethical 'welfare state', there endures an unavoidable tension between the quest for personal independence and the acceptance of interdependence, both necessary constituents of the good life.

Yet, secondly, set against this universalizing quality of impairment and conception of the ethical state in the manner of philosophical Idealism is an awareness of being part of a 'discrete and insular minority', whose shared characteristics create group solidarity and a claim to distinctive status. Such recognition brings with it a sense of the particularity of human experience, of the fine grain of personhood and its individual dignity. The ascription to the human person of civil and human rights provides a counterweight to the importance of the collective as a source of cooperation and shared endeavour.

Thirdly, Massie's evocation of 'team spirit', of the richly diverse contributions of local associations and informal groups, invites the valorization of social movements, and of civil society organizations that enable a measure of active participation, otherwise elusive within larger institutional structures. Echoing the US independence rallying call of 'no taxation without representation', the disability movement proclaimed 'nothing about us without us', an assertion of the virtues, not so much of representative democracy, but of participatory democracy, organizations 'for' disabled people being subsumed over time by organizations self-consciously 'of' disabled people, as expressions of active citizenship.

Finally, in the suspicion of movement politics and of an ideological commitment to a particular 'model' of disability, Massie expresses a 'problem-solving' disposition to social and legal issues that is commensurate with approaches associated with pragmatism. Rather than rationalism and abstract theory, Massie's response to the fact of impairment and disability is rooted in experience and in the practical learning derived from that experience.

These four themes – Idealism, humanism, pluralism and pragmatism – although at times nuanced and even contested, represent significant features of the disability movement and of its contribution to the practical politics of human rights. They are linked also to prioritization of relationships with the state as the enabler of fulfilling human capability, of relationships with the community as the source of overlapping identities and support, and of the notion of the self as the bearer of entitlements that are inherent to human beings and demanding of reciprocal responsibilities. Underpinning those commitments endures the practical problem-solving engagement that has enabled substantive and sustainable achievement in the political and legislative arena.

'A spectrum of human capability'

It was some time after the emergence of disability rights as a concept in the US before the idea came to the serious attention of lawyers in the UK. In 1991, the Institute for Public Policy Research published a manifesto for a new law on disability rights by Ian Bynoe, then legal director of the mental health charity Mind (Bynoe et al, 1991). In their introduction, social theorists and pioneers of disability studies Mike Oliver and Colin Barnes set out for an audience of British policy makers, with an unmistakable air of novelty, the basic principles underpinning the social model of disability. Reflecting on the gains of the civil rights movement in the US, the introduction in the UK in the 1970s of anti-discrimination laws on race and gender, and the increasing assertiveness and confidence of disabled people themselves, the authors sought to minimize the importance of individual limitation in the experience of disability and instead to prioritize the importance of disabling barriers that are social and environmental: discrimination is the result neither of individual impairment nor personal prejudice but of 'the institutionalised practices of society' (Bynoe et al, 1991: 14).

In a pioneering study published in 1994, disability lawyer and activist Caroline Gooding offered a deep reflection on the intellectual and practical implications of the emergence of disability rights as a social movement and campaign for law reform (Gooding, 1994). At the centre of her reflection was insistence upon the inseparability of law and politics (O'Brien, 2016). Gooding expressed resistance both to the idea that law can be conceived as an autonomous social sphere and to the notion that it is irrelevant to political progress. Undaunted by arguments that the demonstrable failure of legal measures entails exclusive reliance, by way of alternative, on political commitment, Gooding argued on the contrary that legal intervention is a 'useful tool and weapon' in the broader political struggle, precisely because of its unavoidably political force. Drawing upon the feminist scholarship of Carol Smart, Gooding emphasized law's functioning as a 'forum for articulating alternative visions and accounts' as an indication of its political potency (Gooding, 1994: 30).

In the case of the struggle for disability rights, those alternative visions and accounts entailed an attempt to transcend the inherent individualism of the law and a move away from the negative prohibitions of the tort model of formal equality, according to which an employer or service provider would incur liability only if personally responsible for harm suffered by an individual claimant. In their place would be the articulation of an alternative model of substantive equality that would enable collective approaches rather than reliance on individualized mechanisms. Even more fundamentally, this process of re-envisioning would invite the rethinking of the meaning of disability itself and of the categories that the language of disability had been compelled to sustain. The neat category of 'disability' masks a fluid and messy 'spectrum' of human capability. In much the same way that radical approaches to sexuality recognize its 'polymorphous' quality, its entanglement in a 'spectrum of shifting objects of desire', so radical approaches to disability should reject the 'social myth' of a 'sharp dichotomy between able-bodied and disabled', made possible only by the forms of production and reproduction associated with industrial capitalism. Such a society not only shapes attitudes to disability but artificially 'constructs a disabling identity into which individuals are fitted' (Gooding, 1994: 45, 9, 13).

'The collective self-organization of disabled people'

The welfare state, despite its progressive potential, had in Gooding's view exerted controlling power over disabled people. It did not require sympathy with the neoliberal assault on the welfare state to consider that its restructuring brought with it an opportunity to redefine the relationship between the state and disabled people, and indeed between the state and citizens more generally. For the realization of that opportunity, it would be necessary to align any 'legal' interventions with the collective activity of the disability rights movement on the ground. Any form of individual rights-based legalism could serve only as a supplement to collective needs-based welfare, whose pre-condition would be an effective social movement. The goal was to 'go beyond the American model and to link up with other disadvantaged groups to defend and extend the welfare state' within a new rights-infused framework of value: 'The most important attribute of the rights ethos is its ability to stimulate the collective self-organisation of disabled people, upon which ultimately the potential for such progress depends' (Gooding, 1994: 173).

The prescience of Gooding's remarks is apparent from the later analysis of disability rights in the US following the passage of the Americans with Disabilities Act (ADA) 1990, which provided the template for the development of rights-based anti-discrimination disability legislation in the UK and across Europe. Despite the emergence of rights-based activism as an alternative to welfarism, the experience of disability rights activists in the meantime was interpreted by some as reinstating the importance of the social welfare system in achieving their goals, not instead of a rights-based approach but as a necessary supplement (Bagenstos, 2004, 2009). Any 'restructuring' of welfare provision must nevertheless 'seek to solve the problems of paternalism and oppression that advocates identified in an earlier generation of disability welfare programmes' (Bagenstos, 2004: 68). The positive value of the state, and the need for positive interventions to promote that value, are according to such analysis essential components of a progressive agenda for disabled people, and for all citizens, who must invariably find themselves somewhere on that spectrum of vulnerability, disadvantage and interdependence that universally characterizes all human experience.

The Disability Rights Commission: responsive legality in action

In search of 'reflexive regulation'

The importance of social movement politics in the reception of disability rights legislation is apparent from the gradual adoption throughout Europe of rights-based legalism as an alternative to needs-based welfarism. It is noteworthy that, although regarded, along with other Scandinavian countries, as a world-leader on equality, especially on gender rights, Denmark was notably slow in adopting rights-based legislation on disability. By the time it passed disability legislation in 2004, and then only in response to the EU Equal Treatment Framework Directive, Denmark had understandably earned the sobriquet of 'disability rights-based laggard' (Vanhala, 2015: 844).

By contrast, Sweden and Finland had enjoyed disability rights provisions in their constitutions since 1974 and 1995 respectively, and the UK had passed the first comprehensive disability-rights legislation anywhere in Europe, with its Disability Discrimination Act (DDA) 1995.

This halting acceptance of rights-based legislation in Denmark can be attributed at least in part to the way in which the disability movement, in keeping with the country's political traditions more generally, considered a 'corporatist approach' to be consistent with the social model's emphasis on 'voice' and 'inclusion'. The Danish Disability Council took a determined line in arguing that rights-based legislation is incompatible with the established methods of cooperation between citizens and state, which had enabled considerable influence for disabled people in policy making in Denmark between 1960 and 1980. A rights-based approach, the Council considered, might be acceptable in the more individualistic society of the US, but not in Denmark where mutual ties and communal solidarity were considered a prominent feature of social and political life.

Denmark's hesitance was nevertheless an exception to the wholesale adoption of rights-based approaches to disability legislation in the EU and North America after 1985. For the most part, the aspirations of disabled people dovetailed with federal and supranational government initiatives to consolidate the legitimacy of hitherto weak centralized governmental structures. This coalition of interests was apparent, for example, in the Trudeau government's constitutional project in the 1980s, which led to the Canadian Charter of Rights and Freedoms 1982 as the first constitutional recognition of disability rights anywhere in the world, with reliance placed on individualized enforcement mechanisms instead of publicly funded state initiatives (Keleman and Vanhala, 2010: 9). It is perhaps noteworthy in this context that in the US the ADA 1990 was introduced by Republican President George H.W. Bush, and in the UK the DDA 1995 by a Conservative government under the ministerial lead of William Hague MP, who was then Minister for Social Security and Disabled People.

It has been argued that in Europe rights-based legalism threatened to undermine the consensus model of democracy as a pathway to 'social Europe' in the 1980s (Keleman and Vanhala, 2010). A mixture of depleted resources and limited political will left law-making the primary tool of the European Commission. The Treaty of Amsterdam (Article 13) 1997, the Race Discrimination Directive 2000 and the Equal Treatment Directive 2000 were significant steps towards the realization of anti-discrimination legislation throughout Europe, with the European Court of Justice serving an equivalent role to that ascribed to the Supreme Court in Canada. This reliance on litigation as a social control mechanism heralded a new era of 'Euro-legalism', but with doubtful benefits for democratic politics more generally (Keleman, 2011).

In Britain, the challenge of evading the snares of adversarial legalism was particularly acute for the DRC, the statutory body established by the Labour government in 1999 to oversee the coming into force of the DDA 1995. The DRC was to be a short-lived experiment, active as a separate organization only between 2000 and 2007, when it was absorbed into a new Equality and Human Rights Commission. Nevertheless, by the time the DRC closed in September 2007 it could be observed that its promotion of the social model of disability and its rejection of a purely formal approach to equality had laid the foundation for the achievement of substantive equality for disabled people across many policy domains (Fletcher and O'Brien, 2008; Vanhala, 2011: 244).

An important precursor to the development of the DRC's approach to law was the publication of the Hepple Report in 2000. The report, 'Equality: a new framework', constituted an independent review of the enforcement of UK anti-discrimination legislation and was based on evidence received from some of the most prominent practitioners in equality law (Hepple et al, 2000). At the centre of the report's recommendations was a prescription of 'reflexive regulation', to displace the dominant 'command-and-control' approach designed for increasingly outmoded hierarchical organizations with a 'top-down, rule-making' ethos. By contrast, 'reflexive regulation' recognized the need to bring into the regulatory process the experience and views of those directly affected, such as trade unions, community organizations and public interest bodies. In the context of equality law, such an approach entailed the development of the positive public sector equality duties that shaped the Equality Act a decade later and turned equality law on its head by shifting the emphasis from retrospective action by aggrieved individuals to prospective action by public authorities, with scope for communitarian engagement in the process of scrutiny on the ground.

The practice of mediation: citizen engagement and 'participative process'

There are four aspects of the DRC's approach to its work beyond conventional litigation and adversarial legalism, forged in the heat of Hepple's reimagining, that warrant further exploration: alternative dispute resolution (ADR); codes of practice; formal investigations; and third-party (amicus curiae) intervention in court proceedings. As early as 1966–7, when the Race Relations Board presented its first annual report to Home Secretary Roy Jenkins, it was emphasized that anti-discrimination legislation should not be thought of in terms of coercion. On the contrary, the Board's early experience reflected the emerging lesson from the US: only in a 'tiny proportion' of cases is it necessary 'to invoke the sanction of the law' because 'the process of conciliation is central to this type of legislation' (Race Relations Board, 1966–7: 21–2).

Uniquely among the UK equality commissions, however, the DRC had statutory powers to arrange for the provision of 'conciliation services' (in practice 'mediation') in relation to goods and services disputes, to supplement the work of the Advisory, Conciliation and Arbitration Service in relation to employment disputes. Experience of equal rights enforcement in the US was salutary: Paul Miller, an adviser to President Clinton on disability and a commissioner in the US Equal Employment Opportunities Commission, drew upon the high percentage of disability cases settled by the Commission through mediation to argue persuasively that ADR could serve as a 'just alternative' rather than 'just an alternative' to the court process (Miller, 2001). In the UK, the experience of the Equal Opportunities Commission (EOC) in sex discrimination cases encouraged support for 'rights-based' ADR, characterized by entirely voluntary participation of both parties, binding and public settlements, and the engagement of specialist mediators who would ensure that the parties were adequately informed of their rights and responsibilities and that any settlement achieved was consistent with the values of the legal framework (Hunter and Leonard, 1997).

The DRC used its ADR powers to create a Disability Conciliation Service, which in two organizational incarnations between 2000 and 2007 handled over 500 cases, of which more than 80 per cent led to settlement. During the same period, the DRC funded fewer than 200 goods, services and education cases in the courts, which saw very few DDA cases at all, in contrast to the employment tribunal where anti-discrimination litigation was concentrated. Apart from the individual resolutions achieved 'in the shadow of the law', the possibility of wider systemic change within the offending organization, of reflection on important issues that were not easily amenable to legal classification, and of more wide-ranging remedy beyond the financial compensation available in the courts, such as changes in organizational practice and commitment to future training, added significant potential to the use of rights-based ADR. Rights-based mediation of this sort offered the possibility of bringing about 'culture change' in public authorities and private organizations in a way that translated abstract rights issues into aspects of everyday life. Just as importantly, it enabled the active engagement of disabled people as citizens in transformative practice: '[I]ncreasing individuals' involvement in vindicating their own rights through participative processes like mediation brings those rights home' (Doyle, 2007: 64).

Statutory codes of practice: an instrument of civic education

It was remarked of the DRC's statutory codes of practice that they were a 'model of their kind' in providing an authoritative interpretation of the law and in reinforcing the DRC's role as 'the guardian of its legislation' (Rubenstein, 2007: 13). A striking example of its approach can be found in its code on rights of access to goods, facilities and services published in 2002, two years ahead of the proposed changes, to allow for a sustained educational campaign before the new law came into force (Disability Rights Commission, 2002). The need for civic education was especially acute since many organizations anticipated those changes with considerable misgivings, the requirement to alter physical barriers to access as part of the DDA's 'reasonable adjustment' provisions being construed as burdensome and unnecessary.

The DRC's code sought to reassure by emphasizing the overriding purpose of the changes as being to give access to services, not to buildings as such. It also alleviated fears by explaining the wide range of available adjustments, many of which would entail little or no financial cost. The underlying philosophy was notably universalist in drawing attention to the way in which changes that would improve access for disabled people would have significant advantages for everyone, not least for that large group of people who, although not 'disabled' within the meaning of the DDA, were nevertheless significantly disadvantaged when it came to accessing essential services. At the centre of such a philosophy was Gooding's idea of a spectrum of ability applicable to all, rather than a restricted label of 'disability' associated with a 'discrete and insular minority'.

'Own-initiative' formal investigation: beyond individual litigation

A third strand of the DRC's work that circumvented adversarial legalism was its conduct of 'formal investigations', which could be initiated without individual complaint and to that extent entailed a wide measure of discretion in the choice of focus, whether specific organization or entire sector. When the Commission for Racial Equality (CRE) was established in the 1970s, the preceding White Paper had made it clear that its formal investigation powers were to be its most important and distinctive, its chief task being 'to identify and deal with discriminatory practices by industries, firms or institutions ... on their own initiative ... and whether or not there had been individual complaints about the organisation investigated' (McColgan, 2000: 293). That the use of such powers proved controversial is a measure of the common law's tenacious hold over the legal imagination and of the primacy afforded adversarial process over anything that has about it so much as a whiff of continental inquisitorial methods. Having completed 16 investigations in its first two years, the CRE was then stopped in its tracks by a series of judicial reviews. Legal heavyweights Lords Hailsham and Denning entered the fray to condemn such investigations as reminiscent of the Star Chamber or the Spanish Inquisition, and as entirely incompatible with British conventions of liberty and fairness (Hepple, 2011: 149–50). As a result, the use of formal investigation powers by the equality commissions was marginalized by legalistic assumptions, until revived by the DRC in 2003.

By then, the DRC was the beneficiary of statutory powers that sought to bypass the negative experience of the other two equality commissions by imposing a time-limit on the conduct of investigations to sharpen focus and by introducing a conciliatory element through enabling agreement with putative subjects in lieu of formal investigation. In addition to several agreements in lieu of enforcement, the DRC completed three investigations during the seven years of its existence: into the impact upon disabled people of website inaccessibility; into health inequalities as they affected people with psycho-social or learning disabilities; and into the significance for disabled people of the way in which the key professions of social work, teaching and nursing were regulated. The senior lawyer who chaired the inquiry panel convened by the DRC to collect and examine evidence on professional regulation noted in retrospect that the 'vast and important opportunities' afforded by the DRC's formal investigation powers went far beyond the limited scope of individual litigation in their ability to identify systemic or institutionalized discrimination, and to propose recommendations for changes in practice (Monaghan, 2007).

Third-party intervention as 'social advocacy'

Finally, in the absence of power to fund or assist directly in Human Rights Act cases, the DRC, recognizing the need to give disabled people a voice in such proceedings, took the unusual step for an equality commission of intervening in such cases where a disability rights perspective would also serve the public interest. In one notable case involving two sisters with profound physical impairments, who needed to be lifted at home but had been denied support by their local authority carers on health and safety grounds, the DRC assisted the judge, Mr Justice Munby, to use a more objective human rights approach based on the overarching value of 'dignity', rather than a comparative equality law approach, as a means of reconciling the parties (Palmer, 2007: 298–300). In the event, the judge was able to oversee a settlement that not only disposed of the case in hand pragmatically but attempted to provide an agreed policy for use in future similar cases.

The use of third-party interventions of this sort as a form of 'social advocacy' and invitation to the court to engage in a 'social conversation' represented another example of the DRC circumventing the constraints of conventionally adversarial litigation, liberal legalism and autonomous legality by bringing to existing adversarial proceedings a public-interest perspective and a measure of detachment from the particular dispute, with the aim of infusing the judicial decision-making process with broader social context and policy implications. Such interventions were in this way a contribution to a more deliberative form of adjudication by the courts, in which public benefit and the common good became part of the judicial equation.

These four features of the DRC's approach to the use of its statutory powers indicate its recognition of the need to avoid reliance for its chief resource on liberal legalism as an aspect of autonomous legality. Significant investment in ADR, purposeful deployment of statutory codes of practice as a form of civic education, and the development of own-initiative formal investigations supplemented by agreements in lieu of investigation and third-party interventions as a form of social advocacy acknowledged the disability movement's historic scepticism about individualistic legal action as a constructive means of changing organizational culture and behaviour, whether in the public or private sectors.

These various initiatives can also be seen as part of the DRC's broader ambition of being 'positive about equality' and of giving force to social rights entitlements, such as rights to education, healthcare, housing and social care, which are not typically justiciable, in the sense of being liable to legal enforcement in the courts. That ambition, rooted in the 'reasonable adjustment' provision, led eventually to the creation of a public sector equality duty on disability, and in the Equality Act 2010 to its extension to cover all protected characteristics (Fletcher and O'Brien, 2008). The former reliance on liberal legalism as a means of control and enforcement had to that extent been superseded by the requirement that public authorities take positive steps to eradicate discrimination, and just as importantly, that they actively engage disabled people themselves in enabling the achievement of that objective.

The UN Disability Convention: returning the 'human' to human rights

Dignity and the 'innumerable bonds of association'

The UN Convention on the Rights of Persons with Disabilities (CRPD), which opened for signature in 2007 after adoption by the UN in December 2006, is confirmation that disability rights, once a latecomer to equality law, has achieved a position of pre-eminence (United Nations, Office of the High Commission for Human Rights, 2007). The first UN convention on human rights of the 21st century, the CRPD realizes many of the ambitions of the disability movement, not least in giving expression to a social model approach and in affirming the positive accent in which it should be enunciated. Gerard Quinn, one of the architects of the CRPD, has written that the CRPD is intended to 'carry the social model of disability rights to the heart of power', embedding it in the 'national architecture' of governance and announcing a worldview (Quinn, 2013: vii). The 'core idea' of that worldview is the acknowledgement that 'humans cannot be reduced to an essence, that we are who we are because of our interactions in community' (Quinn,

2012). The debt to political pluralism for that communitarian perspective is acknowledged by Quinn in his citation of Figgis:

> What is needed nowadays is that as against an abstract and unreal theory of State omnipotence on the one hand, and an atomistic and artificial view of individual independence on the other, the facts of the world with its innumerable bonds of association and the naturalness of social authority should be generally recognised, and become the basis of our laws, as it is of our life. (Quinn, 2012: 36)

As Quinn makes clear, the Aristotelian provenance of the CRPD's notion of freedom encourages respect not for self-sufficiency or uninhibited independence but for 'interdependence' sustained by a sense of participatory belonging and of 'shared, not atomised, personhood' (Quinn, 2012: 40). The CRPD displaces the liberal individualist conception of the rational self, wholly autonomous and self-directing, in preference for a conception of the social self, inevitably constituted by overlapping roles and identities forged in the complex space of civil association, and incorrigibly dependent on mutual systems of support. The CRPD's vision is to that extent one of a shared humanity. Beyond definitions of impairment or disability rests an underlying humanism as the bedrock of what it means to flourish and of the entitlements necessary for all human beings, 'disabled' or not, to achieve that state of fulfilment which Aristotle called *eudaimonia* ('happiness').

Underpinning the communitarian and Aristotelian vision is the concept of dignity, recognized by the chair of the UN CRPD Committee as more prominent in the CRPD than any other human rights treaty, so that 'respect for the human dignity of disabled persons' is quite simply its overriding purpose. Yet the ambition of the CRPD is not merely to describe the world but to change it, to move beyond a statement of human rights law as ideology or morality, as a reflection of political conflict or global power relations, and so to advance recognition of disability human rights as 'a tool for social transformation' (Degener, 2017: 51).

'Transformative equality' and nested governance

In pursuit of that transformational goal, the CRPD Committee has in its General Comment No 6 (2018) promoted a 'progressive' or 'human rights' model of equality, which goes beyond formal equality, and beyond even substantive equality, to prioritize the values of redistribution, recognition, participation and accommodation (Committee on the Rights of Persons with Disabilities, 2018). Its ambition is explicitly linked to a conception of 'transformative equality', which, demanding more than a 'level playing field' or even equality of outcome, has also been proposed as a means of achieving the sustainable development goals for women. Transformative equality of this sort includes among its defining characteristics the redress of disadvantage, the promotion of dignity and worth, the removal of oppressive institutional structures and the achievement of meaningful social and political participation (Fredman et al, 2016).

Significantly, General Comment No 6 also prescribes a means of giving force to its transformative conception of equality that does not rely on adversarial legalism. Instead of viewing monetary compensation as the goal of individual complaint, transformative equality requires 'forward-looking, non-pecuniary remedies' (Committee on the Rights of Persons with Disabilities, 2018: C22). Accountability agencies must as a result have the ability (like the equality commissions of old, and most ombuds institutions outside Britain) to commence an 'own-initiative' inquiry (*actio popularis*), and to deploy a wide range of instruments to achieve changes of culture and perception. Just as importantly, Article 33 of the CRPD prescribes a form of nested governance that transcends conventional styles of judicial or quasi-judicial enforcement: each state party to the convention must 'maintain, strengthen, designate or establish' a 'framework' to promote, protect and monitor implementation. Such a framework must include at least one 'independent mechanism' for coordinating national efforts. To ensure the active civic participation of disabled people themselves, in the spirit of 'nothing about us without us', Article 33(3) insists that civil society, especially disabled people and their organizations, should participate fully in the domestic arrangements for realizing the CRPD's goals, with an Optional Protocol also enabling not just individuals, but groups, to refer alleged violations to the Committee. The Committee may then investigate and make recommendations, like ombuds, which, although not legally enforceable, do require formal response from the states in question.

A new 'normative universe'

As with many human rights treaties, the CRPD is 'programmatic', in the sense that it is 'expressive' of value rather than 'imperative', ethical rather than strictly legal in its authority. As one expert commentator has observed, its most striking potential is 'juris-generative', in the sense that it aspires to the creation of a new 'normative universe' and to 'belief change' regarding disabled people (Lawson, 2018). Its focus is to that extent on 'social imaginaries', 'mentalities' and cultures, hearts and minds rather than legal judgments and legally enforceable remedy. Its success cannot be measured by the number of legal cases brought in national courts or the amount of compensation payable, but by its 'indirect interpretative effect' and its 'bolstering' of existing domestic law with the advancement of 'more progressive interpretations' (Lawson, 2018: 569).

The way in which the CRPD has enabled the creation of this new normative universe is apparent from innovative and communitarian developments in the Indian state of Gujarat (Pathare et al, 2019). Although hindered by a colonial legacy which brought to India an asylum system and 'lunacy' legislation forged in 19th-century Britain (Davar, 2015), in the 1980s the Indian government inaugurated a new progressive era for mental health with the Mental Health Act 1987, which redefined the process for admission and detention. More recently, following India's signing and ratification of the CRPD in 2007, its new Mental Health Care Act 2017 has sought to implement the aspirations of the CRPD. The challenge for the state of Gujarat, as for the rest of India, has been to improve intervention options, including access to anti-psychotic and other medication, but without undue reliance on medicalized approaches at the expense of social, psychological and rehabilitative methods. Additionally, in a setting where social stigma relating to psycho-social conditions has been high, and informal, punitive and restraining interventions commonplace, the larger educational mandate of the CRPD's transformational vision has acquired additional importance.

Even before the passage of the 2017 legislation and the legal changes which followed, the World Health Organization had formed a partnership with a Canadian NGO to launch its QualityRights initiative in 2013 as a framework for human rights reform in line with the approach of the CRPD (Pathare et al, 2019). In the absence of law reform, the CRPD ethos was used to create a shift from a medical model to a recovery-based model of care, with an emphasis on the role and empowerment of those receiving care and on the involvement of those giving care in creating a rights-based approach that was not merely the emulation of individualistic rights-based legalism. In addition to providing a tool for assessing services, improving the service environment and reducing instances of inhuman and degrading treatment, the project aimed to encourage self-help groups, comprising *saathi* (family) groups to provide emotional support and enable family members to participate in their relative's care, and *maitri* (service user) groups to build a network of peers able actively to support each other and participate in planning service delivery. This emphasis on social support and on the communitarian involvement in care of family and 'service user' peer-group volunteers was consistent with the Ahmedabad hospital's existing *aadhar* (support) programme which had been in place since 2011 and which in partnership with the city police and a local NGO had provided a free helpline and additional support for 'wandering persons with mental disorders', many of whom found themselves on the streets because their families could no longer offer support to them in the absence of additional support for themselves (Hospital for Mental Health, Ahmedabad, 2013).

These initiatives in Gujarat are vivid local responses to urgent local need. They are small steps in small places, yet resonant of the values promulgated by the CRPD, even in the absence of prior national law reform. The approaches adopted are multi-faceted, combining enhanced treatment options, individual empowerment, state intervention and community engagement to achieve a measure of change, not without difficulty and at times controversy in the face of competing cultural practices and beliefs. While the basic framework imported from the CRPD is rights-based and still shaped by elements of medicalism, the interpretation of that framework has been far from individualistic or legalistic. The expressive value of the CRPD's provisions, and the conceptual framework which it inaugurated, created a new language in which mental health could be discussed and in which traditional and community resources could be deployed to provide a network of focused support.

The CRPD can be regarded as a human rights treaty of its moment. It is reflective of the achievements of the disability movement over several generations and of the new paradigm of equality that disability rights represent. It is reflective also, and more fundamentally, of strains within the liberal tradition that have been otherwise obscured by legalist dominance, yet which, when reinstated, offer renewed emphasis on the importance of the enabling state, on the resource available in supportive community, on respect for human dignity and on the possibility of social innovation in the achievement of shared problem-solving capacity. It conveys also a message of hope: as the formal evaluation of the QualityRights programme in Gujarat concluded, 'positive change can be achieved within existing legal and policy frameworks even if these are not fully aligned with international human rights standards such as the CRPD', and, crucially, 'even in low-resource settings' (Pathare et al, 2019: 7).

Disability human rights and postliberal response to citizen grievance

The 'new civil rights history'

The implications of the CRPD and the ascent of disability human rights of which it is a part stretch beyond 'disability' to broader consideration of the most effective means of serving the interests of the most disadvantaged and of democratic citizenship more generally (O'Brien, 2022). Those implications are decidedly postliberal. The advent and subsequent elevation of disability within the liberal rights firmament poses a challenge to accepted expectations based on underlying values of individualism and rationalism. Central to disability human rights are notions of the social self, the dignity of the human person, the positive enabling potential of the state, the value of dispersed centres of power and identity, and the need to root theory and practice in 'lived experience' with a view to practical problem-solving. Such emphases expose the limited capacity of the abstractions of political liberalism to respond to the concrete circumstances of everyday life.

In the context of anti-discrimination law, the foregoing consideration of disability rights and of attempts at their realization can be read as one way in which an approach that started in individualistic, adversarial rights-based liberal legalism has tried over time to avoid 'hiding from humanity' (Nussbaum, 2004). By recognizing disability as a spectrum of human experience, by acknowledging its social roots, by privileging the social and communitarian self and by adhering to an overriding vision of human dignity which the state has a positive obligation to uphold, disability human rights have been central to a new paradigm of equality law, which requires enunciation in a positive accent. That positivity finds recognition in the apparently slight but quietly revolutionary concept of 'reasonable adjustment' and in the less bashful mechanism of the positive public sector equality duty. It is a positivity that extends beyond the ethical state to the subscription of civic association, the dignity of human personhood and pragmatic problem-solving initiatives. As such, it takes its place as part of the 'new civil rights history' or 'demosprudence' (Guinier and Torres, 2014; O'Brien, 2016), which is as much about positive social rights as negative civil rights, and which 'places lawyers in conversation with everyday people, social movement organisations and social movements', so that 'law creation' is seen as a 'dynamic and multidimensional process that involves both conflict and collaboration' (Goluboff, 2013: 2320, 2329). That new civil rights history defines the law 'capaciously', resisting the prioritization of case law as pursued in the highest courts, and instead seeking out those lawyers, and non-lawyers, who can play the role of 'intermediaries', 'mediators', 'facilitators' and 'gatekeepers', making connections between 'lay people' and 'formal law', and between 'law and politics' (Goluboff, 2013: 2323).

Towards 'intelligent accountability': the ethical state, partnership, dignity and problem-solving

Disability human rights augur, therefore, a new paradigm of administrative accountability by pioneering interventions that are both demosprudential and precipitously postliberal in their disavowal of adversarial legalism as their presiding spirit and of individualism as their overarching anthropology. When Baroness Onora O'Neill gave her Reith Lectures in 2002 (O'Neill, 2018), she spoke of the need for "intelligent accountability" to replace the dominant culture of accountability which was then, and is still, prevalent, and which is based on the New Public Management values of efficiency and value for money, reinforced by published targets and league tables, and by overreliance on mechanical complaints procedures by which members of the public can seek retrospective redress for professional or institutional failure. While ostensibly promoting a larger measure of accountability to the public, such a regime in fact, she suggested, created a far-reaching system of accountability to a new breed of regulators, exercising a new form of central control (O'Neill, 2018: 52–3). Although the methods of accountability ascribed previously to the disability rights movement have not been complete strangers to New Public Management considerations or legalistic traits in their implementation, they have nevertheless brought into the accountability conversation factors that are at least preliminary to the establishment of intelligent and postliberal accountability.

Those factors touch critically upon the functions of, and relationships between, the state, society and the individual. First, the state is acknowledged, in ways resonant of philosophical Idealism, as a potentially positive and enabling force, neither inherently hostile to the fulfilment of individual potential, nor invariably oppressive in its policy implementation. While entirely realistic about the past failings of the welfare state, its patronising and at times inhumane edges, the prospect of inaugurating that culture of 'bureaucratic humanity' of which Shonfield spoke (Shonfield, 1965: 425) is not lost from view but instead treated as an attainable ambition. The potentially positive interventions of the state are matched by the positive accent of accountability measures designed to establish a clear sense of responsibility, to articulate with authority the constructive interpretation of such responsibilities in practice, and to support with civic education the effective implementation of the recommended practices, while allowing a reasonable measure of discretion and without resorting entirely to individual complaint and enforcement as the primary controlling mechanism. Reasonable adjustments, public sector responsibility, codes of practice and civic education are devices that betray an Idealist conception of the ethical state and its positive function in promoting not just equality but the common good more generally.

Secondly, in the manner of political pluralism, there is the importance attached to the social self, civil society and intermediate civic association in the process of accountability. One measure of that commitment is the need to engage disabled people as partners with the state in the design of services, thereby avoiding any form of passive consumerism in the relationship between citizen and state, but also in the monitoring of the public sector equality duty and the provisions of the CRPD. It is apparent also in the involvement of NGOs, trade unions and other forms of civic association in the coordination of support and in the acquisition of intelligence on the ground that might contribute as a form of social advocacy to public interest interventions in existing litigation, without the limits imposed by adversarial process and by over-identification with the facts of a particular case or set of individual interests.

Thirdly, there is a humanist appeal to an objective standard of human dignity, as opposed to an impossibly abstract exercise in egalitarian comparison, which imports a positive measure of human value that goes beyond formalism or proceduralism. To that extent, disability human rights hold out the prospect of social meaning, a vision of the good life and the good society that is more substantive than the ring-holding neutrality so often associated with political liberalism, its celebration of tolerance otherwise impoverished of positive value. That positive value is not a sanction for enforced social homogeneity or authoritarian rule. Nevertheless, it evokes a communitarian vision that, although receptive to thin cultural ties, is notably more social in its humanist credentials than the atomistic individualism of political liberalism.

Fourthly, the pragmatic strain in disability human rights is evoked by the emphasis on 'lived experience' and the centrality of practical learning that emerges from such experience. The priority of experience and learning translates into a problem-solving approach to law and a participatory generosity to democratic politics as an everyday exercise. It accentuates also the importance of civic education as a pathway to social civility and to 'going on together' as partakers in a common life.

Resonant of the distinctions referred to earlier and drawn by Simon between liberal legalism and a more responsive alternative within the American pragmatist tradition, the background understandings and practices, or ways of proceeding, elicited by disability rights are, as a result, decidedly different from those of liberal legalism and autonomous legality. Active citizenship and a positive role for the state; the recognition of intermediate civic association and the social self; prospective and restorative remedy; more inclusive mediation and deliberative decision-making; and non-adversarial, inquisitorial and problem-solving process: these are the characteristics consistent with a disability human rights approach to the response to citizen grievance. It is an approach that is resonant also of postliberal concerns.

7

Responding to Grievance: Mental Health and Special Educational Needs and Disability

The emergence and consolidation of disability as an indispensable aspect of public philosophy and a catalyst of a new paradigm not just in equality law but in public law more generally provide a fresh and urgent opening for the revival of responsive legality as the defining framework for administrative justice. Yet just as the responsive and incipiently postliberal initiatives in Britain in the interwar and immediate postwar years foundered on the obduracy of restricted, autonomous and legalistic modes of legality, so the ability of a revived responsiveness to exercise its transformative alchemy is diminished by the lure of legalism and the risk of acquiescence in its hegemony. The tension between autonomous and responsive legalities can be illustrated by the way in which citizen grievance is accommodated in the separate but related mental health and special educational needs systems in England. Attention will focus on tribunals and public ombuds as twin institutional centres, before turning to a form of civic mediation which might provide a template for future procedural development.

The 'mental health' context

Mental distress and disability rights: from medicalism to legalism

The situations of those experiencing 'mental distress' or 'psycho–social impairment' were latecomers to the disability rights movement, commonly associated in its early phases with mobility and sensory impairment. The depiction of a wheelchair–user as the readily identifiable symbol of disability access is a recognizable legacy of that emphasis. Although the UN Convention on the Rights of Persons with Disabilities (CRPD) explicitly includes those with psycho–social impairment within its scope, thereby acknowledging the extension of disability rights beyond the categories of mobility and sensory impairment, the recruitment of those experiencing mental distress to the ranks of 'disabled people' has not been without controversy (Spandler et al, 2015). Nevertheless, in the context of the modern history of responses to mental distress, the accession of psycho-social impairment to the disability rights fold has been heralded as largely progressive, as an emancipatory journey from 'patient to citizen' (Sayce, 2000, 2016).

That history is readily disclosed by the waxing and waning of state control within a shape-shifting legal framework, frequently characterized as expressing preferences for 'medicalism' or for 'legalism', respectively, as defining approaches. In a UK context, the high watermark of medicalism is the Mental Health Act 1959, which, despite its creation of mental health review tribunals, reflected an era of 'great optimism in psychiatry', when the advent of new pharmacological interventions held out the prospect of 'cure' for presentations which were regarded as intransigently 'psychotic' (Jones, 1993; Glover-Thomas, 2002: 22–6). By contrast, the Mental Health Act 1983, which replaced the 1959 Act, represents the triumph of 'the new legalism', which had informed the successful campaign during the 1970s of the mental health charity Mind for more effective legal protection of patients' civil rights and of their entitlement to treatment in 'the least restrictive' environment (Gostin, 1983, 2007). Fuelled by the undermining of psychiatry that had attended sociological enquiry at the start of the 1960s, especially in the work of Michel Foucault, Erving Goffman and Thomas Szasz, and by the international movement towards deinstitutionalization (World Health Organization, 2003: 3), the 1983 Act amounted to a significant 'revival of legalism' as a means of exercising control over psychiatrists, with enhanced civil rights protection for those detained and diminished reliance on psychiatric discretion (Glover-Thomas, 2002: 29). Although the 1983 Act created for the first time a right to treatment for those discharged from hospital, the closure of mental hospitals was, it has been noted, hardly matched by an increase in community resources (Jones, 1993).

The mental health crisis in the UK

In the UK, and more specifically in England, the attention drawn to the depleted resources of the mental health system has intensified in the last decade, and especially since the COVID pandemic. In February 2016, the independent Mental Health Taskforce to the NHS in England published 'The five year forward view for mental health' (Independent Mental Health Taskforce, 2016). The picture painted by the review was stark, although no longer surprising in its depiction of the high prevalence of mental distress among the population, among children and young people, new mothers, older people and people marginalized by race, ethnicity, sexual orientation, gender, physical disability or contact with the criminal justice system. Yet while mental distress accounted for 23 per cent of NHS activity across primary care, community services and secondary care, NHS spending on mental health was equivalent to just half that figure (Independent Mental Health Taskforce, 2016: 9).

Shortly after the Taskforce report in 2016, the Care Quality Commission (CQC) published a report in 2017 on the state of care in mental health services, based on its own programme of inspection of specialist mental health services in England between 2014 and 2017 (Care Quality Commission, 2017). While acknowledging that 'the overwhelming majority of NHS and independent services were rated as good or outstanding for having caring and compassionate staff', the report expressed concern about the safety of services, often because of older buildings, limited staff resources and poor management of medication. Despite emphasis since 1983 on the need for patients to be treated in the least restrictive environment, restrictive practices endured, especially in locked rehabilitation wards. Waiting times were unacceptably long and access to services had been curtailed, often because of the decisions of those commissioning services rather than those providing them on the frontline. Clinical information systems were frequently inadequate and reported by staff to be a source of considerable frustration and confusion (Care Quality Commission, 2017).

The CQC's first annual report after the COVID pandemic suggested that things had got worse, emphasizing the continuing need for 'person-centred care', facilitated by 'maximizing patient involvement' in care-planning and decision-making (Care Quality Commission, 2022). The CQC's Lead for Mental Health noted the need not just for increased inpatient bed capacity but rather for the introduction of 'system-wide solutions, including roles to track and review individuals and their care, and a focus on alternatives to admission and facilities for discharge to community services' (Care Quality Commission, 2022: 6). In summary, the CQC enunciated three key messages: 'the workforce is under extreme pressure', 'community services are key to reducing levels of detention' and 'urgent action is needed to address longstanding inequalities in mental health care' (Care Quality Commission, 2022: 8).

The culmination of these various critiques of the current mental health system has been the final report of an independent review chaired by Sir Simon Wessely, published in December 2018, the government's White Paper 'Reforming the Mental Health Act' (2021) and the subsequent publication of a new Mental Health Bill. In the White Paper (Secretary of State for Health and Social Care and the Lord Chancellor and Secretary of State for Justice, 2021), the government has acknowledged the review's findings that the current Mental Health Act does not work as well as it should for patients, their families and carers. As a result, people become disempowered, are excluded from decisions about their own care and treatment and are denied dignity and respect. The legislation, based on the model first introduced in 1959, goes too far in removing autonomy and does too little to protect and support people in influencing and making decisions about their own care. As a result, the government has proposed changes that reflect its four key guiding principles of choice and autonomy, least restriction, therapeutic benefit and ensuring patients are viewed and treated as individuals (Secretary of State for Health and Social Care and the Lord Chancellor and Secretary of State for Justice, 2021).

There are several dominant themes running consistently through these various articulations of the mental health challenge. First, there is an emphasis on the need for targeted support in the community as a means of preventing crisis, addressing disparities in mental health arising from disadvantage and inequality, and enhancing human capability so that people can live more fulfilling lives. Secondly, there is a recognition of the need to harness the positive capability of those who work in the mental health system, including those deployed in in-patient and community settings, and in roles that transgress the boundary between health and social care. An institutional culture that values the worth and dignity of workers, draws upon their insight and experience and enables the exercise of discretion in the discharge of a problem-solving function emerges as a prerequisite of more agile provision. Thirdly, there is the repeated refrain of the need for 'person-centred care', characterized by respect for human dignity and the active participation of 'patients', their friends and family in the design and delivery of support. Such recognition is in part a continuing reaction against the dehumanization associated with medicalism and in part against a form of legalism that has accentuated negative libertarian entitlement at the expense of positive social entitlement.

The SEND context

The context of contemporary 'special educational needs and disability' (SEND) provision is in some ways very different from that of the mental health system. Although, as the experience of Bert Massie described earlier testifies, the removal of children from mainstream society for educational purposes was until quite recently a routine feature of social policy in Britain, its current survival is rarely conceived as a libertarian rights issue. Yet in important ways, the challenges posed by SEND provision are resonant of those in the mental health sector, notably in their convergence on debates about the availability in mainstream settings of adequate 'support', about the recruitment, deployment, retention and morale of frontline staff both in schools and in local authorities, and about the ability of the system to deliver humane practice that is respectful of human dignity, human capability and civic participation.

The Warnock Report (1978) and the Education Act 1981: 'responsible contribution'

When in 1974 Mary (later Baroness) Warnock was invited by then Education Secretary Margaret Thatcher to conduct an inquiry into the education of 'handicapped children and young people', it had been apparent for a long time that provision in Britain was 'less than ideal', and that children in receipt of special education 'were pushed away, out of sight and out of mind', despite the responsibility of Local Education Authorities since 1971 to 'educate', not merely 'care for', all children (Warnock, 2003).

Warnock's personal commitment as moral philosopher and teacher was to a shared vision of advancement of all children towards what she regarded as the common educational goals of knowledge, experience, imaginative understanding and pleasure, and towards active participation in society as 'responsible contributor'. The Warnock Report (Warnock, 1978) replaced categories of 'handicap' with the new concept of 'special educational need', to be judged by multi-professional assessments and formally recorded in a 'statement'. The Education Act 1981 translated much of Warnock's recommendations into legislation and, crucially, affirmed the basic principle that children with special needs should be educated in mainstream settings whenever possible.

With hindsight, Baroness Warnock came to consider that the process of writing a formal statement of a child's special needs ('statementing') as a means of determining provision had been a mistake. In her revised view as first expressed in a pamphlet in 2005, statementing should be abolished because it is 'wasteful and bureaucratic and causes bad blood between parents and local authorities and schools' (Warnock, 2010: 44). Such regrets reflected the widespread perception that the SEND system had since 1981 become a 'battleground' and perennial source of crisis (Harris and Smith, 2011: 51).

Towards inclusion: from New Labour to the SEND Review (2022)

The intervening period has seen a significant measure of reforming activity. The election of the New Labour government in 1997 led to the introduction of a range of inclusive practices, supported by legislative enactment, notably the Special Educational Needs and Disability Act 2001, which strengthened the rights of children with special educational needs to be educated in mainstream schools and was supported by a new Code of Practice. The Lamb Report (Lamb, 2009) nevertheless found that the legal system was still not working as intended. Its findings led to a government Green Paper in 2011, which established new legal rights requiring local authorities and health care providers to 'join up' their approaches and work collaboratively, with all agencies mandated to work in 'co-production' with parents and young people (Hodgkinson and Vickerman, 2009: 118–39; Harris and Smith, 2011: 49–60).

The Children and Families Act 2014 gave effect to much of the Green Paper's approach, extending the legal framework to include children and young people from birth to 25 years old and requiring local authorities to seek information and advice not just from educational professionals but from health and social care practitioners as well.

Official expressions of continuing dismay have nevertheless accumulated, including inquiry by the Commons Education Select Committee and investigations by the Children's Commissioner. Especially revealing of perennial challenges was a 'snapshot' provided by schools' regulator Ofsted in 2021 (Ofsted, 2021). The findings, although based on a limited sample, were acknowledged to be resonant of well-known and widespread difficulties (Henshaw, 2021): the need for better working relationships and 'co-production' between families, schools and local authorities; better support for the 'crucial intermediary role' of the special educational needs coordinator; quicker turnaround times for the production of Education, Health and Care Plans (EHCPs), which replaced 'statements' in England in 2014; reduced reliance upon, or better resourcing of, poorly paid classroom teaching assistants; and less exhausting exposure of families to an 'adversarial and bureaucratic system', already described by the Commons Education Select Committee as entailing a 'titanic struggle' for those trying to circumnavigate its treacherous waters (Ofsted, 2021).

The General Secretary of the Association of School and College Leaders was quite clear in his response to the Ofsted findings: support for SEND is 'critically underfunded', the system for delivering necessary funding 'byzantine in its complexity', and the process for obtaining support through EHCPs 'incredibly time-consuming and bureaucratic'; the process leaves schools 'straining every sinew' to provide what is needed for SEND pupils, but without 'adequate resources' (Henshaw, 2021).

Finally, in March 2022 the Westminster government responded with a Green Paper on provision in England (Secretary of State for Education, 2022). The Green Paper's conclusions suggest that Warnock's lament in 2005 reflects enduring and widely held concerns. Among the proposals made that in part reflect those concerns are the establishment of consistent national standards; the reanimation of the long-held ambition of 'partnership working' and co-production between parents, local authorities and schools; more generous investment in schools and alternative provision; the standardization of EHCPs; and the strengthening of accountability and means of resolving disputes, including by mandatory mediation.

It is notable that, despite the differences in context from the mental health system, the challenge exposed by the SEND system is in important ways strikingly similar. First, there is an emphasis on the constraints imposed by lack of resources and by fundamental systemic considerations that have coalesced over many years to reach current crisis levels. Secondly, there is a series of concerns about institutional culture and resources within schools and local authorities which significantly detract from the ability of the system to meet need, either because of staff shortages, because staff development has been impeded or because staff experience and expertise have not been fully utilized to help solve the recurrent problems which staff are best placed to understand. Finally, there is the abiding need to sustain trusting, respectful relationships between children and young people, schools and colleges, and local authority officers, and to facilitate such relationships by enabling social advocacy and social support.

Responsive stirrings

Not surprisingly, the prevalence of these challenges has generated increasing numbers of grievances about both the mental health system and about SEND. In respect of both, appeals to the mental health tribunal and the SEND tribunal have increased significantly in recent years; in respect of both, the UK Parliamentary Ombudsman and Health Service Ombudsman for England (PHSO) and Local Government and Social Care Ombudsman for England (LGSCO) have responded to increasing caseloads with targeted and thematic reports. Yet the hegemony of traditional legal methods in the development of administrative justice, while clearly not the cause of the substantive difficulties facing mental health services and SEND provision in schools and colleges, have nevertheless inhibited the ability of tribunals and ombuds to achieve their creative potential in these fields. The need for the realization of that creative potential can be identified in three critical areas: the positive activation of the state as an enabling and ethical agent of social rights entitlement and partnership with citizens, the facilitation of civic association as a source of social advocacy, and the realization of human dignity in practices of meaningful participation.

The hub and spokes of tribunal practice

In most liberal democracies, courts and quasi-judicial institutions have been denied an explicit role in social rights adjudication (a notable exception being South Africa) or left at the margins with scope for consideration of 'directive principles' for the allocation of social rights entitlement (for example, in Ireland and India). Denial of an explicit role has been the case in the UK. In the context of the mental health system, the Human Rights Act 1998 and the European Convention on Human Rights have had an impact largely in the oversight of those negative libertarian rights that protect those with psychosocial impairment from unlawful detention, compulsory treatment or other infringements of their liberty. In England and Wales, as in most common law jurisdictions, there exists a complex legislative framework for reviewing detention and the exercise of legal capacity, most particularly in the Mental Health Act 1983 and the Mental Capacity Act 2005. Legislation of this sort has entailed the careful calibration of those circumstances in which those found to have a 'mental disorder' can be deprived of their liberty, forced to have treatment against their will or be denied the right to make decisions about their personal and family life. There exists, for example, in the case of the Mental Health Act, a comprehensive system for review of detention by way of appeal, or in some cases automatic referral, to an independent mental health tribunal, with powers of discharge and, more positively, recommendation, albeit limited to entitlement to leave of absence, transfer to another hospital or consideration by the detaining authority of a community treatment order.

In some jurisdictions, notably Australia, this limitation on the role of the mental health tribunal and the 'rights-based legalism' on which it is founded has been subject to searching critique (McSherry and Weller, 2010). It has been argued, for example, that while there is merit in retaining the core tribunal task of adjudicating on the issue of coerced detention, there is a need to supplement that core function with more 'responsive' powers that relate to treatment access and community care, and with changes in procedure that facilitate social advocacy arrangements and recognition of the role of family and carers. The purpose of such reforms is 'to advance social participation and socio-economic (social citizenship) and civil rights ... at various levels of interaction with governmental or civil society' (Carney, 2010: 261). In this way, the 'hub' responsibilities for monitoring civil rights protection through 'prompt and full interdisciplinary review of involuntary detention' would be complemented by some new 'spokes' which 'fully engage the medical (treatment) and social (functional) implications of care' (Carney, 2010: 272). This combination of 'core and penumbra' features, of a 'hub' comprising libertarian civil rights, and 'spokes' comprising social rights and citizenship, would serve to contribute to a mental health framework that is based on the core value of 'dignity' rather than individual rights (Donnelly, 2010: 274).

It is notable in this context that the Westminster government's draft Mental Health Bill does indeed seek to extend the current very limited power of the mental health tribunal to make formal recommendations. The new bill will enable tribunals additionally to recommend that 'the responsible after-care bodies make plans for the provision of after-care services for the patient'. It has, however, been proposed, for example by the Equality and Human Rights Commission, that the relevant clause should go much further and be strengthened to enable tribunals to identify specific community services, to require a needs assessment within a specified period and to make equivalent recommendations as to how the identified needs should be met (Equality and Human Rights Commission, 2022).

In the SEND context, the role of the tribunal already incorporates positive, forward-looking aspects that aim to shape the local state's commitment to social provision. Instead of a focus upon negative libertarian rights, the SEND tribunal is forward-looking and affirmative. Not merely reviewing a local authority's decision, the tribunal makes determinative orders according to its own judgement of need. In that capacity, it can positively require a local authority to make provision from its own resources, for example to cover the cost of specialist support in a mainstream educational setting or placement in a specialist setting. Following a pilot exercise commenced in 2018, the SEND tribunal has acquired the ability to make recommendations, albeit not enforceable findings, in respect of social care and healthcare provision that is related to the identified special needs of children and young people. To that extent, the SEND tribunal actively intervenes in the allocation of public resources in individual cases, albeit with only limited regard to any broader 'rationing' that might constrain a local authority's decision-making process, and without the ability more positively to address recurrent or systemic issues or facilitate more participatory problem-solving intervention.

Social advocacy: case-conferencing tribunals

The development of participatory problem-solving practice for tribunals has been the subject of extensive debate in a mental health context. It was in the application of mental health law that the notion of 'therapeutic jurisprudence' was first advanced in the 1990s to promote broadly humanistic and holistic approaches to law that would give priority to subjective experience. Such therapeutic approaches focus attention on the styles of forum, information and communication deployed as means of promoting participation; the availability of non-legal representation; and the development of positive powers to address concerns about treatment and community care (Wexler and Winick, 1991). Such 'therapeutic' developments are notably consistent with the disability human rights approach advocated by the CRPD:

> The direction of change that is encouraged by human rights and non-adversarial justice is towards a closer engagement with the needs and aspirations of the people who are subject to tribunal review and, by extension, the perspectives of the families, carers, supporters and services who will be providing support and care to the person. (Weller, 2011: 100)

Such reforms are explicitly an application of the disability movement's philosophy of 'nothing about us without us', an 'expression of a deeper structural transformation in law and society which demands the equal participation of marginalised or vulnerable people and their inclusion in the governance of institutions and systems that are intended for their benefit' (Weller, 2011: 101).

The result is promotion of a challenging and radical 'case-conferencing' mode of tribunal intervention that transcends the dichotomy between medicalism and legalism, and instead extends to reviewing treatment plans and social care arrangements, providing guidance to improve decision-making, monitoring service systems, adopting deliberative and mediation processes and being generally more 'flexible' and less 'court-like' (Carney, 2011). At a premium in such a context are ways of collecting and harnessing complaints data to improve the quality of health care 'at the systemic level' (Beaupart et al, 2014: 505). While further empirical evidence may be needed to demonstrate the long-term impact of such broadly therapeutic approaches, it is already apparent that therapeutic justice offers an important framework for the development of a distinctive form of non-adversarial justice and responsive legality.

Thematic ombud reports and guidance: positive social rights intervention

Since 2018, the combined efforts of the two main public sector ombuds in England, the LGSCO and the PHSO, have led to positive social rights interventions and deployment of more systemic intervention, including in respect of grievances about the mental health system. For example, in 2018 the PHSO published a thematic report on mental health care that attempted to distil the lessons of many complaints investigated that identified serious failings in NHS mental health services. The report noted the importance of the government's 'Five year forward view for mental health' and the CQC's 2017 review of the state of mental health care (PHSO, 2018: 3). In connection with discharge arrangements and appropriate aftercare in the community, it significantly identified a 'huge disconnect between the ambitions set out in the Five Year Forward View for Mental Health' and reality. Far from discharge meeting the aim of ensuring people have the right care at the right time and the support to lead active and independent lives, the PHSO found that discharge planning is often 'rushed, with the patient and their family not involved and little thought given to the support needed in the period after leaving hospital' (PHSO, 2018: 26).

More recently, the PHSO and LGSCO have offered guidance to practitioners on aftercare provided under s.117 Mental Health Act 1983 that draws on their innovative joint working across the health care and social care divide. The key messages drawn from their joint investigations reiterate the need for rigorous assessment of care needs on discharge in accordance with the Care Programme Approach which is an overarching system for coordinating the care of people experiencing mental distress. Emphasis is placed on the need to put in place support that will reduce the likelihood of future detention in hospital and avoid delay in provision after discharge, with ample opportunity for early review that includes the participation of the beneficiary of support and of other 'relevant parties'. The need for clear joint-working arrangements is also identified as paramount (LGSCO and PHSO, 2022).

In respect of SEND provision, the element of affirmative intervention available to the SEND tribunal in the allocation of a social right entitlement is complemented by the ability of the LGSCO to investigate complaints about certain aspects of the SEND process and to report thematically on systemic patterns of inadequacy, albeit in the absence of powers of 'own-initiative' investigation: although the LGSCO does have power to extend its scrutiny to matters brought to its attention during the course of its investigation but not explicitly part of the original complaint, it currently lacks the ability to commence an investigation outright without prior complaint and on a public interest basis, and so lacks the formal mandate, funding or internal structures to enable the fully strategic use of an own-initiative power. Since the demarcation between a complaint and a dispute warranting appeal is notoriously unclear, the division of responsibility between the tribunal and the ombud is neither integrated nor 'user friendly'. Nevertheless, the LGSCO has in recent years, for example, addressed local authority delays in dealing with applications for SEND provision, finding fault in 80 per cent of cases, and, more affirmatively, published a good practice guide comprising a suite of recommendations on how to 'get things right' (LGSCO, 2017).

Returning to the issue in 2019, the LGSCO now found itself surveying a 'system in crisis', characterized by severe delay, poor planning, poor communication, inadequate partnership working and lack of strategic oversight (LGSCO, 2019: 2). Significant also was the LGSCO's observation that in some cases local authorities were erecting additional barriers to services in efforts to ration scarce resources. Indeed, as the LGSCO made clear in an evidence session on the SEND Review before the Education Select Committee, the problem is not 'unkind bureaucracy' but lack of resources (Doyle, 2022; Education Committee, 2022).

Thematic reports of this sort by the LGSCO are supplemental to the more routine investigation of individual complaints upon which they are based. In completing those investigations, the LGSCO can make findings and recommendations ranging from individual apology and compensation to full audit of educational provision. Although unable to conduct 'own-initiative' investigations, as already indicated, the LGSCO has been able since 2007 to extend an investigation to cover concerns that come to light even if not identified by specific complaint. To that extent, the constraints otherwise imposed by the empowering legislation are relaxed, enabling a broader reach to the LGSCO's otherwise tightly prescribed remit.

Problem-solving: civic mediation

In the case of SEND, but not the mental health system, there is, in addition to the involvement of the tribunal and the ombud, a fundamentally important additional possibility of engagement of parents and young people in the process of mediation (Doyle and O'Brien, 2020: 113–14). It is a resource that holds out deliberative and transformational potential with acute resonance for postliberal and responsive practice.

Mediation has been available in SEND disputes since 2001, when the Code of Practice articulated the need for local authorities to offer 'dispute resolution services' to the parties. The anticipated benefits of mediation were the more creative exploration of possible outcomes; more sustainable outcomes resulting from more trust and ownership; better communication about the underlying issues, ancillary to problem-solving practice; and a 'tiered' process that is iterative and enabling of worked-through differences (Doyle, 2019: 14).

Since the reforms of 2014, there has existed an obligation on the part of parents and young people in most cases to obtain a 'mediation certificate' before bringing an appeal, to confirm that information about the possibility of mediation has been received and the option of mediation considered. If the parent or young person decides to request mediation, the local authority is obliged to attend and at a sufficiently senior level to enable a decision to be made without reference back to the local authority's authorizing panel.

Mediation usually entails a face-to-face meeting between the parties, with potential participation from school or college representatives, local authority social care teams, a clinical commissioning group in respect of health issues, and other educational and legal professionals, as required. The mediation itself is facilitated by an independent trained mediator, with the aim of discussing the issues and reaching agreement and resolution, if possible. The cost of the mediation will be borne by the local authority, although the mediation-provider must be independent of it. It has been observed, most importantly, that

> unlike mediation in civil and commercial disputes ... in the SEND context mediation does not prioritise a 'full and final settlement' but instead prioritises collaborative problem-solving in a way that allows for expression of the parties' different, and often conflicting, needs and interests. Even where mediation does not result in an agreement, it provides an opportunity to clarify the issues in dispute ... and help

narrow the focus of the dispute if it proceeds to a tribunal hearing. (Doyle, 2019: 13)

Such obligations have accompanied a significant increase in the number of SEND mediations, from 75 in 2015 to 5,900 in 2022, although the measurable impact on outcomes is unclear. There is, for example, suspicion that as the numbers have increased, so local authority commitment to the process has declined, with cases coming to mediation that should have been dealt with earlier and more locally, and with local authority preparation and representation at mediations being diminished in quality (Doyle, 2022).

If mediation is to fulfil its potential and be deployed more widely in emerging settings other than SEND, for example in disputes about health and social care, education, decision-making in the Court of Protection, and tax, its claims to civic rather than merely consumerist credentials require renewed emphasis (Boyson, 2020; Salem and Doyle, 2023). A model of consumerist mediation derived from practice in commercial settings where confidentiality is at a premium, self-interest the assumed motivation, 'compromise' the expected tactic and 'business as usual' the desired outcome is likely to be perceived as a 'private' and 'negotiated' form of justice that is inappropriate in situations where what is at stake is public provision and human rights. Unlike a more 'solidaristic' citizenship model based on values of cooperation, equal outcome, social justice and cohesion, a consumerist model will tend to value individual competition, choice and markets. Failure to look beyond such a consumerist model to an approach rooted in citizenship leads therefore to an impoverished account of the potential of mediation as a participatory and deliberative forum entirely appropriate to disputes about public resources and social rights, and in which 'responsibility', not 'choice', is the value 'central to the participatory dimension of citizenship' (Harris, 2011: 27).

The commonly held view that mediation can serve as a quick and cheap alternative to litigation is misleading. Its true potential depends instead upon the skilful deployment of time and expertise, and the development of trusting constructive relationships. In the absence of such features, mediation is ill-equipped to secure the sustainable transformations that might otherwise serve as a genuine alternative to the 'assembly line of complaints and appeals that the administrative justice "system" increasingly resembles' (Doyle, 2022).

The continuing constraints of liberal legalism
Responsiveness denied

The reviews into both the mental health system and SEND published in 2021 and 2022 respectively are indicative of the perceived crises that beset both. In neither instance has administrative justice or the function of response to grievance attracted sustained analysis or been presented as a significant part of the solution, despite in each case proposals for relatively marginal tribunal reform. In the case of SEND, the proposal of 'compulsory' mediation not only offends against the widely held understanding that mediation must be voluntary if it is to be meaningful but suggests a continuing preference for a quick and cheap form of consumer mediation primarily as a means of reducing tribunal backlogs rather than as an instrument of civic and transformative intervention. The existing scope of tribunals, ombuds and mediation remains constrained, with the role of tribunals 'not particularly effective' at enhancing the quality of decision-making by public authorities (Adler, 2010b) and largely restricted to deciding whether regulations have been applied correctly by officials, not whether any broader form of justice has been achieved. With their role limited to that of adjudication, tribunals serve as the instruments of policy, but without scope for detecting patterns of structural failure, for offering systemic feedback or for exercising a responsive and purposive impact on public administration. It has been observed even of the SEND tribunal, for example, that although in theory inquisitorial, 'the appeal process itself still has an inherently adversarial character, with the parties adopting individual positions and having to respond to each other's case' (Harris, 2011: 84). As the Lamb Report observed in 2009, 'many parents are finding appeals too difficult and complex and feel unable to pursue their claim without legal support' (Lamb, 2009: 5.80; Harris, 2011: 84).

In both mental health and SEND contexts, tribunals, and even the less formally 'legal' forums of ombuds and mediation, are limited in their ability to respond to any of the priorities consistently identified in the social contexts they habitually encounter: the positive role of the state in facilitating delivery of resources, the value of frontline workers in drawing on their expertise and experience to develop solutions to problems, and the capacity of civic association in enabling the full participation in problem-solving of aggrieved but socially embedded citizens. The result is the endurance of practices and processes that frustrate the 'responsiveness' of administrative justice and the democratic agency of citizens on either side of the street–state divide.

The enduring lure of legalism

On either side of that street–state divide, the traces of recalcitrant legalism endure, frustrating response to changing social realities. On the street, the reality is that citizens who have contact with the mental health system or SEND are not social atoms devoid of social context nor are their grievances isolated social phenomena, either from the perspective of the aggrieved citizen or that of the street-level bureaucrats who encounter them. Yet the legalist approach to doing justice insists on the artificial division of social experience into separate singularities, obscuring through its inherent individualism the fact that injustice is invariably multifaceted and 'clustered'

(Clements, 2020). The insistence that legal problems be considered in isolation, in other words, denies the reality that 'the law is political and so too is lawyering' (Clements, 2020: 16). Procedural 'individuation and differentiation' is one of the trademarks of autonomous legality, yet an indicator also of legalism's inability to respond fully to social need.

On the state side of the street–state divide, the New Public Management has in recent decades sustained organizational cultures that combine prescriptive rules and compliance techniques with incentive-based targets, leading to the stifling of innovative problem-solving by those on the frontline. The challenges facing both the mental health and SEND systems disclose the impact of such cultures on the creation of, and response to, grievance. In such a context, the use of individual complaints as a method of identifying lapses and as part of a culture of compliance can too easily become a source of demoralization for frontline workers and of disillusioned frustration for those aggrieved (Clements, 2020: 80–3).

The consequences of such a culture are not confined to the mental health and SEND contexts. A report commissioned in 2010 to investigate failures in child protection offers instructive illustration (Clements, 2020: 84–6). The author, Professor Eileen Munro, identified as a key problem the 'over-bureaucratised nature of the system' and a 'process led approach' intended to 'stop people making mistakes'. Such an approach deployed three distinct mechanisms of control: 'psychological pressure on professionals to try harder', 'reducing the scope for individual judgment by adding procedures and rules' and 'increasing the level of monitoring to ensure compliance' (Munro, 2011). As Luke Clements observes (Clements, 2020: 86), the report endorsed a finding of the House of Commons Health Committee that 'most harm was not done deliberately, negligently or through serious incompetence but through normally competent clinicians working in inadequate systems'; what was needed was 'deeper understanding of why professionals have acted in the way they have, so that any resulting changes are grounded in practical realities' (Health Select Committee, 2009).

Such observations were echoed more recently, and in respect of a superficially very different administrative context, by Wendy Williams' review of the 'lessons learned' from the Windrush scandal, which had found the Home Office seeking the deportation of British citizens as a result of a series of administrative errors (Williams, 2020). Home Office culture was 'dominated by targets', where 'meeting service standards is like a religion' and where staff 'somehow lived in a kind of bubble where the most important thing was how many files you got through'. Echoing the classic analysis of street-level bureaucracy as activity marked by considerable responsibility but hardly any power or discretion, the review noted that '[c]aseworkers also find themselves in a system that requires them to make a large number of often life-changing decisions but denies them the autonomy more senior staff would enjoy'. In summary, the entire organization was characterized by a 'focus on volumes and targets, which manifests itself in sometimes unsuitable, impersonal language when dealing with cases and performance, and which has lost sight of the person at the centre of each case' (Williams, 2020: 104, 134–44).

Jettisoning the luggage

The mental health and SEND tribunals serve important appellate functions in providing much-needed safety nets for those who are aggrieved by relevant state institutions and state actors. The initiatives of the PHSO and LGSCO, including their joint work in respect of mental health care, can be seen as significant attempts to transcend the traditional legal approach identified as an obstacle to doing justice, not least by exercising in a limited way the critical function of identifying patterns of systemic failure. Mediation, of the citizenship rather than consumerist sort, offers transformative possibility. Yet the conclusion is hard to resist that such agencies are themselves disadvantaged in the task of doing justice by the constraints of legalism. Such an approach privileges civil rights entitlement at the expense of social rights. It maintains a strong strain of individualism that competes with and frequently obscures any attempt to identify and remedy repeated patterns of failure and the clustering of problems. It discounts the value of social advocacy by those other than the individual aggrieved person, reinforcing methods of soliciting information that are instinctively adversarial. Its repertoire of options for enabling the active and meaningful participation of those aggrieved is seriously circumscribed, by custom even when not by law. In its inclination to maintain clarity and one-off enforceability, it struggles to concede much discretion to workers or to solicit their constructive, and iterative, engagement in active problem-solving. Its conception of remedy is dominated by retrospective redress rather than prospective restorative and affirmative possibilities.

Despite the prospect of an alternative held out by disability human rights, responsive law and postliberal values, the expectations created by a tradition of autonomous legality and liberal legalism remain hegemonic, even when under social pressure. Alluring still is a social imaginary characterized by the individual victim perspective, populist suspicion of public institutions and the prioritization of individual, negative, civil rights. It is a social imaginary underpinned by traditional ways of proceeding that are individualized and differentiated, organized by reference to rules, and highly sensitized to privacy, confidentiality and adversarial control of information. In the words of Arundhati Roy, quoted earlier, the pandemic is a 'portal', and this post-pandemic era a gateway to something new. In an administrative justice context, the luggage that must be jettisoned to enable easy passage and the envisioning of another world includes these still dominant understandings and ways of proceeding (Roy, 2020).

8

Postliberal Administrative Justice

Disability human rights invite transgression of the traditional legal approach to citizen grievance against public authorities. In the mental health and special educational needs and disability (SEND) systems, ombuds, tribunals and mediators have accepted that invitation while being constrained from doing so effectively by the residual constraints of legalism. The Weberian model of compliance still casts its shadow, obscuring the complexity of street-level bureaucracy, of socially embedded citizenship and of intelligent accountability.

An alternative that is responsive to social reality takes account of postliberal strategic emphases: on the positive enabling function of the state and the delicate moral equilibrium of the street-level bureaucrats who embody it; on society as a positive network of empowering association and identity; and on the individual citizen as endowed with dignity and political agency by formation in the complex networks of that civic association. Against that background, the function of those agencies charged with responding to citizen grievance becomes one of orchestrating the bridging relationships between citizen, society and state so that damaging social relationships are transformed into sources of mutual restoration.

The state and therapeutic justice

The limitations of 'administrative justice'

The illustrative material afforded by the mental health system and SEND has indicated that the barriers preventing innovation are frequently 'structural', entailing political considerations about the allocation of public resources, and 'systemic' in that they concern the way in which public authorities are organized and run. As the ethnographic literature on street-level bureaucracy indicates, they are 'cultural' also, concerning the ethos and texture of institutional relationships, both internal and external. Such challenges are not confined to the mental health system or SEND but extend across much of the public administration fabric: recent studies, for example, of the 'hostile environment' in which immigration policy has been implemented by the

Home Office, and the 'cruel, inhuman and degrading' application of benefits sanctions by the Department for Work and Pensions, reinforce the need for approaches that go beyond the 'usual suspects' of more mass complaints-handling and individual retrospective redress (Adler, 2018; Thomas, 2022).

In principle, and to some extent in practice, ombuds are better placed than tribunals and mediators to address such political, systemic and cultural factors. As previously noted, however, despite the generous aspirations in the 1960s for the ombud as an agent of a new culture of bureaucratic humanity, the consignment of the ombud to a legal and constitutional niche has, as Crick predicted in the 1960s, left ombuds, in England at least, at risk of being a vehicle of legalism, albeit of a more subtle variety than that of the court system (Crick, 1965). What is now designated as 'modern ombudsman practice' represents an alternative to command-and-control approaches to accountability that is in danger of merely reinforcing incentive-based New Public Management standards and principles, and of being limited to consumerist values of customer-care and transparency (Gill et al, 2020). Managerialism of this sort and the celebration of 'the managerial ombudsman' neatly coalesce with compliance models of accountability and their heavily inflected legalism (O'Brien, 2020).

Proposals for making changes to the design of ombuds and tribunals have nevertheless gained increasing urgency, addressing in part the repeated calls for the need of 'culture change' in public authorities, especially those perceived as 'oppressive', such as the Home Office and the Department for Work and Pensions. A far-reaching study of immigration administration has, for example, welcomed the Windrush Review's detailed recommendations for culture change within the department, engagement in more robust and inclusive policy making, and a more inclusive workforce (Thomas, 2022: 268). Yet as the author also sanguinely observes, the likelihood of full implementation, given the department's track record on responding to adverse findings since 2003, is slim, especially since many of the recommendations require long-term structural, systemic and cultural change. As far as 'legal remedies and controls' are concerned, the study concludes from its preceding analysis of tribunal appeals and judicial review challenges that such legal controls are essential and 'to a large degree' effective. Nevertheless, the redress system is creaking at its seams: appeal rights that are necessarily rationed, limited scope for courts and tribunals to address the underlying problems and 'unjust and oppressive behaviour' which goes beneath the radar and cannot be expected to yield individual remedy every time. The study proposes in response 'the development of new forms of administrative control': the adoption by the department of positive ways of correcting errors and managing casework; addressing 'systemic dysfunctions' that cause 'oppression' by developing 'an ethos of administrative empathy' rather than simply opting for 'just more remedies'; creating an external agency that 'works collaboratively' with the department; and extending the role of the Parliamentary Ombudsman to include own-initiative investigation powers and 'detailed scrutiny' of the department's casework and enforcement systems (Thomas, 2022: 268–79).

Similarly, a study of welfare benefit administration has concluded that the use of sanctions by the Department for Work and Pensions amounts to 'cruel, inhuman and degrading treatment', for which the only real remedy will be replacement of a 'bad system' with a better one. 'Softening' the regime by reducing discretion, introducing standard questions to be asked by 'work coaches' before making referrals to decision-makers, specifying in regulations what constitutes a 'good reason' for a claimant failing to comply, introducing 'warnings' and 'provisional decisions', all of which are recognized as improving 'administrative justice' in the decision-making process, hardly pass muster as sustainable solutions of the systemic problem (Adler, 2018). The implication is that 'administrative justice', while desirable, is incapable of addressing the underlying issues and of doing anything to remedy the cruel, inhuman and degrading treatment on occasion meted out to welfare claimants by public authorities. As remarked of the immigration system, the options for reform remain 'inevitably conditioned by the real-world pressures and demands of politics and administration' (Thomas, 2022: 268).

Systems-thinking, localism and culture of innovation

It is such realization that has increasingly drawn attention to the 'fire-watching' and 'fire-prevention' potential of administrative justice institutions as a necessary supplement to their 'fire-fighting' capacity (Harlow and Rawlings, 2009: 528–69). It is the aspiration for that more systemic intervention that has also grounded the ambition for ombuds, in particular, not just to 'put it right' but to enable public authorities to 'get it right' and for governments to 'set right' the network of accountability agencies as a fourth 'integrity' branch of the constitution (Buck et al, 2011). Calls for more explicit filtering powers to enable ombuds to develop strategic focus, to conduct own-initiative investigations, to cascade learning about complaint handling to public authorities in the role of a 'complaints standards authority', and to exercise more extensive reporting powers aim to push ombuds beyond their current functions and develop their ability to create cultural change in the public authorities within their remit (Kirkham and Gill, 2020). Less obviously, but just as importantly, the realization of the poor match between purpose and resource informs the calls for 'holistic' approaches to administrative justice and for 'joining up citizen redress', including, crucially, by a measure of localism that, in England at least, might disperse to the regions the oversight of dedicated local ombuds (Dunleavy et al, 2005, 2010). In that way, they might 'get to know their patch in detail' and 'deal directly with their manageable sub-sets of public sector organisations on a recurring basis, so as to improve lesson-drawing and to spread good practice in more effective ways'; at the same time, there would be more chance of retaining closer relationships with local citizens and a more visible presence, even if such reforms come at the cost of being seen by some in 'the redress sector' as 'attacks on vitally important civil liberties', which are perceived as residing exclusively in the ability of individuals to pursue their personal rights-based claims (Dunleavy et al, 2010: 452).

These various proposals in their different ways draw attention to the importance of systemic environments within and between public authorities. The development of 'systems thinking' as an antidote to command-and-control approaches seeks to foster a 'culture of innovation' to replace the established 'culture of compliance' (Seddon, 2008). To enable that cultural shift, systems thinking seeks to banish wasteful compliance regimes that tie up workers' time in writing specifications for standards, guidance, targets and reporting schedules, in fearing and being on guard for inspection, in developing dysfunctional ways of achieving compliance that in practice diminish rather than enhance competence, and in experiencing the demoralization attendant on the denial of reasonable autonomy. Instead, it celebrates the freedom of street-level bureaucrats to exercise discretion and responsibility, and to find their motivation not in the carrot or the stick but in the pride that goes with the dignity of work well done and the skilful exercise of occupational craft. This approach is an alternative to that of command and control yet one that does not take refuge in marketized incentives or transparency as panacea. It offers instead an environment, a 'new architecture', that 'liberates public servants from the prison of suspicion and distrust that the current regime locks them into, demeaning their professionalism with simplistic targets and casting them as self-interested producers, as part of the problem rather than part of the solution' (Seddon, 2008: 197).

A new environment of this sort is in turn built on a positive view of human nature and the dignity of work, and on the belief that 'people are motivated more by pride in their work than by money, that they are vocational ... and that they are capable of using their own ingenuity and initiative' (Seddon, 2008: 197). It asserts also that cooperation is more fruitful than competition and that since people's behaviour is a 'product of their system', it is only 'by changing the regime that we can expect a change in behaviour' (Seddon, 2008: 197). As Clements has summarized the challenge, making public authorities open to the insights of systems-thinking requires that 'they reject managerialism as an administrative system and in so doing that they commit to a continual process of improving their organisations' "culture" by ... listening to and empowering their frontline workers' (Clements, 2020: 106). It is a process in which administrative justice agencies must also participate if they are to contribute competently to their 'systemic' ambitions.

In the context of the argument advanced in this book, all such proposals should be read as incipiently postliberal in that they shift emphasis away from the individual as victim, from the populist assumption that the state is 'the enemy', and from the assertion that individual civil rights are trumps. Against such a social imaginary, these alternatives reinstate the centrality of the empowered citizen, the resource of social connection and civic association, and the subordination of abstract and individualized rights to the purposive and practical activity of shared problem-solving in the service of the common good.

Counter-hegemony, 'virtuous scheming' and the moral economy of street-level bureaucracy

The need for a shift in social imaginary of this sort is accentuated by other work ancillary to administrative justice scholarship that in its ethnographic turn lays bare the inner workings of public authorities and the complexity of street-level bureaucracy. It is only by engaging with that complexity that external agencies such as ombuds, tribunals and mediators have any chance of realizing the elusive goal of 'culture change'. The assembly of research around the notion of 'legal consciousness' has drawn attention to how precarious is the hold in practice of 'law' and rules on street-level bureaucrats. Far from supporting the belief that strong external control, authoritative adjudication and rigorous legal enforcement will achieve positive impact, such work suggests that 'legal compliance is not all about authority and enforcement but is also dependent on frontline officials' own beliefs and expectations' (Hertogh, 2010: 222). At street-level, fully committed 'legalists' are outnumbered not just by those who are less enthusiastically 'loyal' but by those whose 'cynicism' is based on informed dissent and by those whose 'alienation' is rather more visceral and uninformed. It is not necessary to go so far as to suppose that law's hegemony is so entirely displaced that it becomes in effect 'nobody's law' (Hertogh, 2018). It is sufficient to note that at street-level there is at work a 'counter-hegemony' that finds expression in 'resistance', 'murmurings' and 'ruses' (de Certeau, 1984), in 'virtuous scheming' (Paquet, 2009), in the local exercise of phronesis and of resourcefulness (*metis*) (Scott, 1998; Zacka, 2017).

This is the ambience of street-level bureaucracy evoked by Zacka's ethnographic report from his fieldwork in a US welfare counselling department (Zacka, 2017). His insights are especially salient to the democratic dimension of street-level bureaucracy in action and to the displacement of a Weberian style of 'compliance' from its central place in accountability regimes. Zacka proposes as a basic framework for democratic public agencies the fundamental values of fairness, efficiency, respect and responsiveness. Of these values, only efficiency is shared to any significant extent with private agencies, for whom the strictures of democratic value are not directly relevant. Importantly, the precise moment of 'decision-making' is not the only, or even the most significant, aspect of a bureaucratic process that inevitably engages emotions as well as thought for its proper functioning.

In the construction of state–citizen encounters, the moral perceptions and role conceptions of street-level bureaucrats are, according to Zacka, critical but subject to 'reductive takes on the role' or 'pathologies' that represent 'adaptive response to the pressures of everyday work'. These key pathologies Zacka identifies as 'indifference', 'enforcement' and 'caregiving': indifference represents the classic bureaucratic malaise of alienation, finding expression in a shoulder-shrugging 'it's not my problem' attitude; enforcement by contrast represents zealous commitment to standards and consistency, a determination to ensure that no one gets away with anything because of exercises of discretion that might also be construed as rule-breaking; finally, caregiving denotes an over-identification with the predicament of the individual citizen and the assumption of the role of 'saviour' in a way that stretches the street-level function beyond its limits (Zacka, 2017: 66–110).

To counter these pathologies, Zacka detects in the approaches of street-level bureaucrats what he describes as 'a gymnastics of the self' that entails careful self-examination in response to feedback; calibration of responses by dampening and heightening identified tendencies or habits; modulation, by way of the moderation of sympathies and antipathies; and moral perception, as a way of reinforcing appropriate boundaries (Zacka, 2017: 140–51). One of the chief tools at the disposal of street-level bureaucrats in this ascetic enterprise is 'everyday casuistry', in the sense of that style of reasoning that enables engagement with the particularity of the situation encountered, an ability to adopt a flexible and revisable approach without undue constraints imposed by precedent-setting or precedent-following, and a measure of realism rather than subservience to policy or unbending principle (Zacka, 2017: 167–71). Such 'tactics' in the exercise of discretion are especially important when 'the rules run out', or, as Robson put it, when public servants are faced with those 'imponderables' for which there is no readily prescribed answer (Robson, 1928).

Purposive intervention: orchestrating 'organizational phronesis'

Zacka's account of the way in which the moral economy of street-level bureaucracies is constructed offers the basis for identifying the distinctive quality of a postliberal form of accountability that can address the state as 'partner' and public authorities as 'collaborators' in a common participatory purpose. Zacka does not explicitly address the potential role of administrative justice agencies, ombuds, tribunals or mediators in such a scheme of accountability. We might add to his observations, however, the conclusion that administrative justice agencies should indeed be enlisted in the task of preserving the fragile moral ecosystem of public bodies. Critical to the exercise of accountability of this sort is the fostering of a working environment in which 'a plurality of moral dispositions can develop, and in which individual workers are sufficiently committed to their own ways of inhabiting the role to act as lively advocates for them' (Zacka, 2017: 184). 'Peer-level accountability' is in practice the central means by which such an environment can be established, entailing invariably a diversity of moral dispositions within it to match the pluralism of democratic society. In the interplay of these respective dispositions rests a form of moral reasoning that amounts to organizational phronesis and acceptance of organizational responsibility for that virtuous activity, both cognitive and affective. Yet as Zacka emphasizes, reliance on such informal styles of accountability cannot be pursued in isolation. Instead, they should serve as 'supplements' to other channels of accountability and so constitute part of a 'plural regime of accountability', so that 'even as peers police each other, it is important that clients keep reporting behaviour that they find unacceptable and that they have adequate channels to do so; that supervisors keep asking questions and continue intruding occasionally on discretionary spaces of their subordinates; and that professional communities keep probing and overseeing the behaviour of their members' (Zacka, 2017: 195) – and we might add that administrative justice agencies contribute constructively with their own distinctive style of orchestration.

Critical to the exercise of such an 'orchestrating' function will be purposeful engagement with street-level bureaucrats themselves, not just their line-mangers and superiors, who are more likely to follow the 'official' line and less likely to betray the tendencies to cynicism and alienation, the reductive pathologies that disturb the necessary equilibrium. At the heart of such engagement will be the establishment of sustainable relationships that can generate mutual recognition and trust. It is in the construction of such relationships that localism and the dispersal of power is at a premium, so that, as previously observed, those engaged in the task of orchestration can 'know their patch', spot patterns of recurrent difficulty, get a feel for institutional texture and frame interventions so that they land as intended.

Citizen and state: a new relationship

The expectation of 'customer care' has become a familiar feature of contemporary consumerism. Less noticeable has been reciprocal concern for the dignity and engagement of those who are the object of citizen grievance. Yet it is just as important that those who work for public authorities should be the beneficiaries of an ethic of care, of effective communication and engagement, and of consistent recognition of their dignity. At the core of such reciprocity is a form of 'therapeutic jurisprudence' (Wexler and Winnick, 1991) that takes seriously the 'dysfunctional' and anti-therapeutic impact on street-level bureaucrats of traditional ways of responding to grievance, and that entails a 'paradigm shift'. That shift has been described as an exercise not so much of putting new wine in an old bottle but of making a new bottle altogether (Gill et al, 2019: 663–4). Such a shift would entail a 'non-adversarial paradigm' that deploys 'the sensibility of mediation' (Doyle and O'Brien, 2019: 114–17) and problem-solving techniques, and is oriented towards future outcomes rather than retrospective redress; it would emphasize alignment between citizens and street-level bureaucrats in a shared project of democratic citizenship and rely upon processes that are deliberative and inclusive rather than adjudicatory and exclusive; it would express the value of participation in public governance and support conceptions of the 'relational', 'collaborative' or 'partnership state', in which citizens and state officials have an equal stake.

It has been suggested that such a paradigm shift is unrealistic, not least because it would entail a 'significant reconceptualization of the relationship between citizens and the administration' (Gill et al, 2019: 658). Instead, on this account, it is necessary to settle for measures that would 'soften' the rough edges of the traditional approach, retaining its 'antagonistic character' but improving procedural fairness and communication. That softening approach would have the advantage of being 'fairly uncontroversial' and fitting well with good practice 'already recognised in the complaint handling literature', albeit with the novelty of extending an ethic of care and of therapeutic justice to those complained about as much as to those doing the complaining. Such would be the ambition of 'therapeutic complaints resolution' (Gill et al, 2019: 664). It has been the contention of this book, however, that emergent postliberal politics already entail a 'reconceptualization of the relationship' between citizen and state, such that the relationship, if it is to be conducive to the common good, should no longer be conceived as one of antagonism, of victim and oppressor. Moreover, as the recent studies of immigration and welfare benefits have suggested in ways which reinforce the identified barriers to responsive governance in mental health and SEND, formalism and proceduralism are not sufficient to the task in hand of reinforcing democratic citizenship in the service of the common good. Taking refuge behind the strictures of a residual legalism and autonomous legality is no longer feasible. Instead, approaches that are responsive to a postliberal environment are necessary if 'governance' and 'accountability' are to touch the nerve of organizational culture and help maintain its democratic equilibrium. It is the failure to grasp that painful nettle that is more likely to prove unrealistic.

Bridging social distance: 'social conversation' and 'participatory readiness'

If one half of the responsive legality equation is a more focused attention on the purposive improvement of public authorities and the state in the interests of competence and the common good, the other is a reciprocal release of human potential and capability residing in ordinary citizens who have grievances about their everyday interactions with the state, whether local, regional or national. That realization of potential can be construed in part as the need to engage a wider range of participants in response to grievance as a form of 'social conversation' rather than a primary exercise of adjudicatory power. It has been said of the notion of legal adjudication as a form of social conversation that it

> de-centres the judicial role itself, portraying litigation not as a transfer of hierarchical power to the court but as a trigger for democratic interaction between judges, government actors, and different social and political groups. Groups with a voice in the political process are able to enter into the conversation and shape its outcome. (Fredman, 2008: 100)

Public interest litigation: an exercise in social advocacy

Exploration of such conversational possibilities has been notable in attempts to make formal court proceedings a more democratic forum for considering social rights issues, such as those arising from health, social care, housing and educational contexts. It has been observed that 'instead of re-ploughing the well-worked terrain which ranges justiciability against non-justiciability, the real challenge is to formulate a democratically justifiable role for the courts'; the prospects of meeting that challenge are after all made more promising by the fact that 'courts need not have non-revisable powers; nor are they necessarily bound to procedure which is adversarial, costly, slow and unable to deal with polycentric questions' (Fredman, 2008: 100). The reforms introduced by the Supreme Court in India as a means of facilitating the development there of 'public interest litigation' (PIL) are a striking example of attempted democratizing reform (Divan, 2016). In a programme of innovation since the 1980s aimed at release from the 'blinkered rules of standing of British-Indian vintage', the court has, for example, enabled the regular intervention as a third-party in litigation of NGOs in an *amicus curiae* capacity and as an exercise in 'social advocacy', where public reasoning rather than interest bargaining is the primary mode of discourse; the commencement of court proceedings by way of informal letter rather than formal process; and the adoption of more inquisitorial methods of investigation by the appointment of special commissioners to establish the facts in a public interest case. To provide remedies that are not merely compensatory and retrospective, the court has shown a preference for the device of 'continuing *mandamus*' as means of procuring restorative remedy, with the court having responsibility for keeping the case open and insisting on regular progress reports on compliance. As the court has itself said of PIL, litigation of this sort 'is not litigation of an adversary character for the purpose of holding the State ... responsible for making reparation, but it is a public interest litigation which involves a collaborative and co-operative effort ... for the purpose of making human rights meaningful for the weaker sections of the community' (Fredman, 2008: 126–8).

Such developments have not been without critique, especially from those who have detected the gradual subservience over time of the voices of the poor in such conversations to those of more articulate and better resourced citizens. For such critics, the Indian experiment in informal or *panchayati* justice has singularly failed to achieve its transformational potential, amounting to little more than an 'ideological attack on Anglo-Saxon institutions', later 'overlaid with the global cool of Alternative Dispute Resolution' (Bhuwania, 2017: 137). Yet considerable claims have nevertheless been made for the achievements of PIL in India, not least in extending access to free school meals for children, in getting more children into school in the first place, in promoting affirmative action as an antidote to discrimination and more generally in responding to fast-changing social perspectives on matters such as sexual violence and sexual identity (Ganguly, 2015).

Polycentric governance: deliberation and participation

In the context of public administration, street-level bureaucracy and administrative justice, the challenge remains one of how everyday intervention by tribunals, ombuds and civic mediators can, in ways far removed from judicial review proceedings in the High Court or set-piece public inquiry, contribute constructively to social conversations of this sort that further the prospect of deliberative practice. The form of structured social conversation that has most obvious alignment with the ethical, relational and partnership state is likely to be one based on participatory, decentralized and deliberative democracy. Related ideas on governance have emerged in the discussion evoked by Elinor Ostrom's Nobel Prize-winning explorations of the 'commons' as a focal point for a renewed form of civic engagement (Ostrom, 2012). In work to develop the idea of the 'urban commons', attention has turned to a 'nested governance structure' in which those making use of services work cooperatively with public agencies and public officials to design, monitor and give force to the norms established to help manage shared resources. This new style of 'polycentric governance' aims to bring together public, private, social and civic actors, alongside 'knowledge institutions' such as universities, in collaboration with the state, whose primary function becomes that of enabling civic participation and upholding democratic values. The city of Bologna is one focal point for such commons-based experimentalism, creating a juridical framework for shared social and urban rights, including entitlement to participate in the creation of the city, to be part of the decision-making processes shaping citizens' lives and to contribute to decisions about the use of collective resources in which all citizens have a stake. Such initiatives constitute a 'collaborative pact for organised legality', which is democratic, non-partisan and community-based, and at the same time a source of urban commons governance and organization (Foster and Iaione, 2016).

Within a polycentric governance model of this sort, the function of responding to grievance when things unravel devolves to intermediaries capable of maintaining the practices of participation, deliberation and decentralization. Such practices will in turn entail supportive scaffolding as a means of structuring sustainable social conversations. That scaffolding has been identified as including methods to engage all participants inclusively, the design of principles for managing process and making decisions, determining appropriate representation and expert input, ways of fact-finding and gathering information, the ability to monitor implementation of outcomes, and above all a style of discourse that is commensurate with shared democratic citizenship (Menkel-Meadow, 2006: 18–22).

From such scaffolding issues the prospect of meaningful participation, rather than mere consultation, through the deployment of expert and empathetic facilitators and without any coercion of the parties, who must remain willing participants in the process if a sustainable outcome is to be achieved. Such a process is not possible without cooperative interaction with public authorities and a process of reasoned deliberation leading to decisions that will in many instances be contingent and revisable (Menkel-Meadow, 2006: 18–22). At the same time, if such deliberative processes are to be 'scaled up' to address issues of embedded disagreement about health care and social care entitlement, housing and educational provision, they must take account of emotions as well as self-conscious thought, affective considerations as much as cognitive, so that deliberation is practised in its 'passions mode' as much as its reflective mode (Menkel-Meadow, 2011).

'Role literate participants' and the maintenance of complex space

There is a critical role in such practices for a facilitator who is capable of 'making conversation' in the first place and deploying expertise and experience to make such conversations as fruitful as possible as an exercise in 'consensus-building' (Menkel-Meadow, 2004/5). As 'role literate participants' (Guinier and Torres, 2014), institutional agents such as tribunals and ombuds, as well as civic mediators, in ways appropriate to their distinctive functions, bring to the task the ability to coordinate, bridge and reinforce a diversity of perspectives that might enable fruitful problem-solving and organizational learning. Moreover, the discharge of that function by ombuds, tribunals and civic mediators can rightly be regarded also as an exercise in 'the rule of law'. It is 'the rule of law', however, interpreted according to the ancient Aristotelian conception of 'the rule of reason', rather than a modern notion of 'the rule of rules' or 'the rule of rights' (Shklar, 1987; Loughlin, 2000). According to that ancient conception, the rule of law is 'essentially a political idea' that requires those engaged in deliberative decision-making to exercise the virtue of phronesis; and the 'single most important condition on which the rule of law rests is that of the worthiness of character of those engaged in legislative and judicial decision-making' (Loughlin, 2000: 70). It is, in other words, the conception of the rule of law that underpins that humanist approach to virtue politics that puts at its centre not codes and constitutions, regulations and penalties, but character and government by people rather than rules.

This recalibration of accountability as responsibility represents a postliberal response to the task of helping maintain the democratic pluralism of public agency. It is moreover a recalibration that reinstates the mutual interplay of the ethical state, civil society and the socially embedded human person as irreplaceable elements of its political cosmology. Instead of the flattening of social space occasioned by the liberal yet binary juxtaposition of collectivist state and atomized individual, postliberalism reactivates a form of complex space that has room for a diversity of intermediary institutions that in turn shape the diverse identities of modern citizenship. It becomes in this context one of the primary functions of administrative justice agencies, such as ombuds, tribunals and civic mediation, to maintain that complex space, uphold the rule of reason and sustain the responsible exercise of phronesis by public agencies and the street-level bureaucrats who work in them.

'Bridging skills', 'participatory readiness' and the arts of democratic citizenship

According to political philosopher Danielle Allen, citizenship is 'the activity of co-creating a way of life, ... of world building' (Allen, 2016: 35). Central to this exercise of citizenship is 'disinterested deliberation' about problems which concern the polity and are to that extent 'political'. The exercise of citizenship far exceeds the limited function of being an 'informed voter' and requires a deliberate schooling in what Allen describes as 'participatory readiness'. Participatory readiness comprises three main elements: verbal empowerment, democratic knowledge and a developed sense of 'the strategies and tactics' that make possible effective action in the public realm. Drawing on the work of fellow classicist and philosopher Josiah Ober (Ober, 2005) in disclosing a new and richer understanding of the inner workings of classical Athenian democracy (notwithstanding its notable exclusionary defects), Allen is at pains to establish that participatory readiness, including the component of democratic knowledge, is not an abstract idea, the mastery of theory or the product of book-learning. It is instead a craft-skill, learned and reinforced through democratic practice. To explain the notion of democratic knowledge, Allen deploys the concepts of 'bonding' and 'bridging' used by Robert Putnam in his studies of 'social capital' accumulation in urban America (Putnam, 2000). As Allen explains, 'bonds' are those ties we form with others because of geographical proximity, ethnicity, religion or similarity of interests. Such bonding is instinctive but potentially exclusionary. For it to be made inclusive or 'cosmopolitan', it must occur in ways that help preserve a shared democratic ethos. The critical question for a democratic society becomes 'how we can bond with those who are like us so as to help us bridge even with those who differ from us' (Allen, 2016: 42). The answer provided by Allen is that bonding of this sort is cultivated by the exercise of 'bridging skills', in the sense of bridging social and cultural difference as a 'science and art of association', practised in democratic contexts that are always relational. Bridging skills of this sort are quite simply 'the capacities by which a translator, a mediator and an individual who can surmount social difference can convert a costly social relationship into one that is mutually beneficial to both parties' (Allen, 2016: 41).

The task of creating 'participatory readiness' for effective engagement in the process of responding to grievance can be seen as an exercise in bridging skills of this sort. It is an exercise of bridging skills by a 'role literate participant', someone who knows the ropes, in a way that both realizes such skills as exemplary practice and extends their use by a practical form of civic education. Responsive intervention by tribunals, ombuds and civic mediators can best be conceived as precisely the work of a bridging institution of this sort. By building upon natural bonds of association and shared patterns of life and experience, such 'bridging' interventions establish a practice of democratic citizenship in which the parties to a grievance participate and are the beneficiaries of facilitated expertise. In short, tribunals, ombuds and civic mediators are invited to practise a form of deliberative democracy in which they make real what they symbolize, namely the art of democratic citizenship.

Postliberal strategic emphases: an overview

By way of overview, it is now possible to summarize the main strategic emphases that emerge from the foregoing considerations in this and earlier chapters, and to identify by way of illustration practical examples of what such emphases might entail. That previous discussion makes it clear that detailed prescription of operational considerations or indeed the promulgation of a set of principles, still less rules, would hardly be compatible with the postliberal and responsive approaches described. Nevertheless, it is possible to identify several broad 'strategic emphases' to be encouraged within administrative justice that are compatible with a postliberal approach to citizen grievance and that distinguish such an approach from liberal legalism. Those strategic emphases in most instances reflect or enhance existing possibilities for innovation, yet their precise application across forums as various as ombuds, tribunals and civic mediation will inevitably depend upon specific circumstances beyond the overview proposed here. The focus remains the interlocking relationships between state, society and individual citizen within a network of institutions characterized as those of administrative justice. In some cases, the changes needed to realize the realignment of emphasis are subtle and incremental; in others, there is a need for structural change, and in yet others a change of style, culture or mentality. The cumulative effect of such re-emphases would nevertheless represent a fundamental shift in modes of response to grievance rather than merely hygienic cleansing or 'tinkering' at the edges. Above all, it requires a change in mentality from the easy assumption that the primary, indeed only, characterization of administrative justice institutions is that of 'redress mechanism' or 'dispute resolution'.

The state: public authorities as vehicles of democratic agency and problem-solving

The first cluster of re-emphases concerns the overarching purpose of enabling public authorities and the street-level bureaucrats who work in them to function with discretion as vehicles of democratic agency, to engage in the 'virtuous scheming' that maintains the moral economy of street-level bureaucracy and so participate in relationships with citizens that are sources of mutual transformation. Instead of the liberal-legalist suspicion of the state and prioritization of individual civil rights, the postliberal alternative will emphasize the positive responsibilities of public authorities, including those deriving from the rebalancing of civil rights with those social rights with which they must be integrated. There will be an attendant determination to share knowledge about the nature of those positive responsibilities, including the social rights entitlements from which they spring, and the more fine-grained implications for the positive construction of good complaint handling and good administration, rather than the mere condemnation of bad. Grievance-mechanisms, as aspiring agents of institutional phrónesis, will be motivated to engage with public authorities in co-producing innovative approaches to meeting those obligations, to acquiring intelligence about the steps needed on the ground, and to monitoring developments. Such determination entails therefore a spirit of partnership in the context of a broader recognition of the partnership or relational state as a vehicle of the common good. The ambition will accordingly be the achievement of restorative remedy both in response to individual grievance and to the identification of systemic incompetence or malfunction.

Consistent with these emphases will be all those options for enabling the detection of patterns of structural failure and impoverished organizational culture, the accumulation and promulgation of shared learning, practical engagement with street-level bureaucrats as well as managers, and the purposive pursuit of active enquiry rather than passive reaction to those individual grievances that happen to percolate to the top of the pile. The co-production of practical guidance that is useful, proven to be usable and shaped by practical experience and active engagement with 'grass roots' delivery; the ability to initiate inquisitorial investigation and assembly of information, and thereby get under the skin of public authorities; and the desire to develop partnerships and cooperative, non-adversarial approaches with public authorities: all these steps will underpin an ethos that is pragmatic and above all problem-solving. Response to grievance will therefore entail in the first instance a mandate of influence, not sanction.

The purpose of such a mandate is not the usurpation of the function properly assigned to the executive of delivering public services, nor that properly assigned to industry regulators of setting detailed regulatory regimes within which entire sectors must operate. The purpose is instead to enable administrative justice institutions to serve as bridging agencies between individual citizen, street and state, and to do so with a measure of deliberative creativity otherwise denied them by overidentification with legalistic aspirations.

As earlier discussion has indicated, recent work, in theory and practice, has already contributed positive steps in this strategic direction. Most striking has been the increasingly vociferous calls for public ombuds in the UK to acquire own-initiative powers of investigation, so that they can finally transcend the 'small claims substitute' role and so play a more purposive part in the development of good public administration. Such calls are not new: as long ago as 1978, Harlow was advocating what she envisaged as an 'inspector-general of administration' role for the ombud, which would shift the focus of attention from past bad administration to future good administration (Harlow, 1978, 2018).

In the absence of explicit own-initiative powers, the steps taken in England by the Parliamentary and Health Service Ombudsman (PHSO) and the Local Government and Social Care Ombudsman to promote principles of good administration and to develop better means of delivering constructive feedback to public authorities through thematic reports and annual reviews of performance can be seen as concrete examples of entirely feasible shifts of emphasis. In Scotland, the Scottish Public Services Ombudsman has in recent years acquired powers to oversee complaints handling in public administration with a new 'complaint standards authority' function, which emphasizes the positive purpose of supporting the design and implementation of good systems for responding to citizen grievance (Gill, 2020a). At the same time, the public ombuds in Wales and Northern Ireland have for the first time had the benefit of legislative reform to enable them to conduct own-initiative investigations as a deliberate extension of their public interest remit (Gill, 2020b).

Meanwhile, comparative research has demonstrated the benefits of own-initiative powers in addressing the needs of groups otherwise rarely heard, in focusing attention on issues of exceptional importance and public interest, in contributing to public debate and deliberation, in accessing much-needed data (Creutzfeldt, 2020) and in prompting law reform (Diez, 2018). Ombud practice in the Netherlands, for example, has reinforced the importance of the ombud monitoring recommendations made, of engaging constructively with public authorities through processes of regular liaison, of using a varied palate of desk research, case review, citizen outreach, stakeholder roundtables, staff secondments, targeted questionnaires and in some instances the establishment of a temporary public hotline on a particular issue (de Langen et al, 2018).

This ethos of strategic opportunism offers a credible rebuttal of those 'red tape', 'mission-drift' and 'rogue-ombud' objections made to own-initiative powers by some (Gill, 2020b). It is moreover consistent with exhortations for administrative justice institutions more generally to move beyond an 'accountability model' of regulation to a 'learning model' that holds out the promise of genuinely systemic improvement (McBurnie, 2022). Such a revised model puts at a premium the need for administrative justice institutions to shed their image of being distant and remote, and instead to become the owners of productive conversations and relationships with the public bodies within their jurisdictions. That emphasis on relationship, anticipated in the 1940s by Morris Jones, has reinforced the importance of a clear and common language, of making defensive behaviour unnecessary and of a shared vision of better public administration (McBurnie, 2022). Such changes are part of that broader shift towards therapeutic modes of justice referred to earlier, whose larger ambition is the release of participatory energy in the practice of deliberative decision-making.

Society: civic association as a source of social advocacy

The second cluster of re-emphases concerns the ambition of supporting and enlisting civic association in the task of responding to grievance, thereby expressing and reinforcing the values of the connected society as nested community, in which difference is successfully negotiated and a viable modus vivendi achieved. Such engagement recognizes, as for example in the development of public interest litigation in India cited earlier (Fredman, 2008), the socially embedded quality of the individual person, the inevitability of multiple identities, perspectives and horizons, and the benefit of shared experience and expertise.

At a premium therefore will be the possibility of enhancing forms of social advocacy, including the targeted engagement of peer-group representatives, voluntary sector organizations, carers and family. In some cases, such an approach will entail a model of response that might be described as a form of case conferencing, as proposed in Australia as a function of the mental health tribunal (Carney, 2010, 2011), where the multiplicity of voices reflects the complex social space in which clusters of problems arise and which otherwise evades the grasp of processes that are marked by bipolarity and the dissolving of complexity. In the UK, such forms of social advocacy can already be found in the practice of the PHSO. For example, in 2009 the voluntary sector organization Mencap played a coordinating role in giving expression to shared perspectives in the Six Lives investigation into the deaths of people with learning disabilities in national health care (O'Brien, 2011, 2013). Indeed, the then UK Parliamentary Ombudsman, Ann Abraham, explicitly recognized her office's 'mandate of influence' and its inherently iterative and inclusive process as 'an exercise in deliberative democracy ... a dialogue between citizen and state that is mediated and even facilitated by the Ombudsman' (Abraham, 2009; O'Brien and Thompson, 2010).

This style of deployment of social advocacy in what Sandra Fredman has described as the 'social conversation' of deliberative decision-making indicates more broadly the way in which postliberal administrative justice, whether in the work of ombuds, tribunals or civic mediators, already has available to it a suite of flexible processes and procedures that are incipiently deliberative. As Carrie Menkel-Meadow has emphasized, the success-criteria for deliberative democracy as practised in the context of response to citizen grievance will be met by the active participation of the fullest range of interested parties, and by the use of inquisitorial techniques to acquire high-quality information, evidence and data; by the deployment of conversational strategies that enable full participation and critical enquiry; by the co-production of ground rules freely consented to; by the iterative practice of conditional and amendable decision-making; and by the monitoring of practical implementation of decisions deliberatively agreed (Menkel-Meadow, 2006). In these various practical ways, administrative justice agencies can discharge their function of 'role-literate participant' and 'architects of participatory democracy' in processes to which the other participants will be largely strangers (Menkel-Meadow, 2004/5).

The individual: democratic citizenship and meaningful participation

The third cluster of re-emphases, directed at promoting a form of democratic citizenship that is active and meaningfully participatory, is in effect a specific application of the broader aspiration towards social advocacy just considered, albeit with the focus on the 'participatory readiness' of the individual citizen as one among several potential participants. Such an approach requires more than the sometimes rather rudimentary expectations of a passive form of inclusivity that merely pays lip-service to information provision and consultation. The practice and development of democratic citizenship entails more positive reinforcement of human dignity, autonomy and agency. Relevant, certainly, will be the provision of accessible information and support, but necessary also will be that higher level of participatory readiness that approximates to a form of civic education.

With the benefit of participatory readiness, those approaching grievance-mechanisms will be equipped to participate in a democratic forum that is deliberative, problem-solving and therapeutic. One model available for adaptation to such practice will be mediation, but mediation that conforms to the values of citizenship not consumerism. Civic mediation of this sort should not be assumed to represent a quick or cheap option. It will instead entail preparation and practice that is iterative and aimed at more than immediate closure and business as usual. It will require cooperation, not coercion, and skilful facilitation. It is moreover a 'sensibility', a capacity for 'accommodating many voices', that is complementary to a wide range of grievance-response mechanisms, capable of working in tandem with ombuds and tribunals, and of informing their habits of mind and practice (Doyle and O'Brien, 2019: 114).

The application to administrative justice more generally of techniques and approaches forged in the practice of civic mediation represents a practical form of non-adversarial justice that is therapeutic, restorative and problem-solving. It has been argued that such approaches represent a form of 'participation plus' that is more than just 'empowerment' and instead rooted in the philosophy that underpins the UN CRPD, namely 'nothing about us without us' (Weller, 2011). Such an approach entails more than the provision of information or of legal representation. Instead, it looks to a broader range of practical measures to facilitate meaningful conversations between equals and the deployment of advocates drawn from community, lay and peer groups (Weller, 2011: 97). In short, the change that is encouraged by non-adversarial justice is one of closer engagement with the needs and aspirations of those whose grievances are under consideration. Such engagement recognizes that justice is invariably 'clustered'. It recognizes also that individual identity is always complex, shaped by social forces and expressed through the habitual engagement of families, carers and other sources of formal and informal support in daily life. The aspiration towards 'nothing about us without us' expresses the need for equal democratic participation in the governance of institutions and, as a result, the need for ways of enabling such participation that transcend options that are doggedly individualistic or rooted in legalistic styles of thought.

Administrative justice: integrated but dispersed, problem-solving, bridging institutions

The final cluster of re-emphases will make possible the achievement of these various strategic objectives by creating an overarching approach to citizen-grievance that is integrated. Meaningful integration will need to dissolve the legalistic distinction between complaint and appeal, enable the registering of grievance through apparatus that is centralized, in the sense of comprising a single portal, but dispersed, in the sense of actively allocating grievances so registered to the appropriate channel, that will in turn be sufficiently porous to transgress formal boundaries and enable problem-solving that is genuinely holistic. Such integrated, but dispersed, features will hold out the prospect that the grievance system itself is not only more easily navigable but capable of creating narratives that are meaningful in the context of everyday life. To achieve that end, the practical delivery of interventions will be local, in emulation, for example, of city and regional ombuds in federal jurisdictions such as Canada and Australia, so that familiarity breeds trust, not contempt, and competence that is visible rather than remote and largely out of sight (Dunleavy et al, 2010). The postliberal prescription is to that extent one of 'small is beautiful', without the liberal legalist assumption that centralization, universalization and uniformity are the invariable conditions of democratic response to citizen grievance.

The overarching ambition of such reconfigured systems will be to enable the everyday operation of grievance-mechanisms – ombuds, tribunals, civic mediation – as bridging institutions, with the purpose and practice precisely of surmounting social difference and converting costly social relationships into relationships between citizen and state, street-level bureaucracy and public authority, that are mutually beneficial and that serve not individual self-interest but the common good.

Such aspirations to holistic and integrated response to citizen grievance find concrete illustration in what has been described as 'the new administrative law', especially as developed in Wales (Nason, 2019). In a challenge to 'traditional hierarchical structures for holding the state to account', new administrative law encourages approaches that are 'multi-disciplinary, pluralistic' and that 'emphasise horizontal collaboration ... and citizen engagement with administration' (Nason, 2019: 703). Sceptical of both common law administrative law in the ordinary courts and of the European approach of administrative courts applying general codes of administrative procedure, the Welsh approach has relied upon 'integrity institutions', such as ombuds, and 'quasi-political institutions' with powers of systemic remedy, as an expression of commitment to social rights and to the view that good administration is a civic good. By-passing traditional court structures, such approaches are 'ostensibly designed to further social and economic equality, with public bodies (including redress providers) required to collaborate, to integrate their activities and to involve the general public in their decision-making' (Nason, 2019: 703). The postliberal ambition of 'catalysing cultural change within public bodies and civil society' is at a premium, rather than the creation of legal rights for individuals to enforce duties through the courts (Nason, 2019: 704).

Postliberal strategic emphases: the case of school exclusions

The practical significance of the tension between postliberal strategic emphases and those of liberal legalism can be illustrated by brief reference to an administrative justice predicament that, although an everyday occurrence, discloses the differences of approach that remain vividly in tension.

The exclusion of pupils from school is part of the everyday life of families even when their own children may not be the subject of direct intervention. Behaviour in schools and its impact on shared learning in the classroom is a perennial concern. The issue of exclusion has attracted mounting controversy since the late 1990s, when what had previously been seen as a matter entirely at the discretion of individual schools and their head teachers became focused more insistently on the rights of the child liable to exclusion and the need for a process in handling disputes that meets the 'fair trial' requirements of the Human Rights Act 1998. Of particular concern has been the recognition that school exclusions disproportionately apply to pupils with special educational needs, to children in care, to children in ethnic minority communities and to schools in areas of economic deprivation.

The most recent statutory guidance on school exclusions gives a flavour of the dense statutory framework which, in addition to human rights and equality legislation, is now relevant to school exclusion. Notwithstanding the complexity of legal context, the overall approach to regulation in education remains 'reflexive' in its acceptance of the limited role that law can play in bringing about change in 'sub-systems' that are inevitably closed to external 'normative intervention' (McCrudden, 2007). Yet for some, reliance on 'soft' measures such as more guidance is deemed inadequate to the task and a poor substitute for rigorous law reform that would pay greater heed to protecting pupils' rights than preserving the autonomy of schools (Ferguson, 2021).

A traditional legal approach to improved regulation and accountability, rooted in a liberal-legalist mentality and prioritization of an exclusively 'redress function', is reflected in proposals made in November 2019 by a working party convened by the legal policy organization Justice: mandatory training on law for senior teachers; better guidance for senior teachers to ensure their decisions are 'more systematic and consistent' and 'meet all statutory requirements'; the creation of a new specialist 'independent reviewer' to replace review by governing bodies, which were deemed to be ineffective and lacking in independence; and replacing the second-stage review by an Independent Review Panel with appeal on the merits to a new first-tier tribunal with powers to remake the decision afresh and direct mandatory reinstatement. The new process would be complemented by increased availability of independent legal advisers and by new statutory guidance comprising 'templates, checklists and model procedures to structure and achieve as much consistency as possible in all key decisions in the exclusion process' (Justice, 2019: 70).

The Justice recommendations were in response to a government review, the Timpson Review, which had adopted a notably different approach (Secretary of State for Education, 2019). It identified four factors as contributing to current practice: differences between school leadership teams; insufficient support for schools in managing disruptive behaviour; the absence of incentives to be more inclusive when the practice of inclusion is likely to entail increased expense and negative performance against the current testing regime; and the lack of scrutiny to prevent schools from avoiding the formal exclusion process. Its 30 recommendations were aimed at helping schoolteachers 'set clear and high expectations of behaviour and outcomes for all children' and at putting in place support for individual children. These aspirations would be realized by investing in the skills of teachers, by removing perverse incentives to exclude or 'off-roll' children who 'might not positively contribute to a school's performance or finances', by continued regulatory vigilance in identifying 'concerning patterns' of practice, and by better sharing of data.

The government, picking up the reflexively regulatory baton offered by the Timpson Review, has since produced revised statutory guidance in September 2022 which is aimed at promoting transparency and providing 'information' to enable schools to use suspensions and permanent exclusions 'appropriately'. The specific changes include better sharing of data and information, better participation of pupils at each stage of the process and better vigilance from governing boards over the level of pupil moves in their school and the demographic profiles of those pupils permanently excluded. There are, however, no fundamental changes to the process of exclusion nor to the legal tests to be applied at each stage (Department for Education, 2022).

The Timpson Review and the revised statutory guidance largely reinforce what has been described as the reflexive quality of educational regulation, with a mixture of guidance, transparency and incentive, and avoidance of the sort of judicialization represented by the Justice proposals. The strategic emphases of a postliberal response as previously outlined would ambitiously, but realistically, transcend exclusive focus on the response to grievance as a 'redress function' and would instead entail measures and considerations different from those of Justice and additional to the Timpson Review or the government's guidance.

First, a postliberal emphasis on the positive duties of a partnership or relational state would seek explicitly to frame interventions in terms of shared social right entitlement to education as an aspect of the common good. The language of shared social entitlement rather than either individual rights or accountability would help shape an emphasis on the broader systemic aspects of school exclusion and the need for problem-solving solutions that are restorative, holistic and forward-looking rather than individualistic and retrospective.

Secondly, the lessons of systems theory and of socio-legal research on the clustered character of 'legal' problems would place at a premium insight into the 'big picture' of disadvantage and the practical need to make connections between different parts of a holistic system that are positive and integrated. While welcoming the active engagement of governing boards as part of the review process and recipients of relevant data, a postliberal approach would emphasize the role of governors as community representatives with a specific democratic mandate which looks beyond the self-interest of a particular school. It would seek ways of taking account of broader environmental considerations such as the 'high stakes accountability' regime for schools, dominated by performance league tables, and the fragmentation of the school system that creates competition for those league table positions and for high exam results and Ofsted assessments. Such considerations would extend to the impact of the reduced function of integral local authorities, academization and the cuts to SEND funding that limit individual support.

Thirdly, against that background, it would pay particular attention to the inherently conflicted role of head teachers and of other school staff as street-level bureaucrats. It would seek ways of engaging them and their trade unions in the sharing of practical expertise and the co-production of solutions, both in delivering positive outcomes for pupils and in enriching the process for responding to grievance. The available research suggests that most teachers recognize that there is a problem with permanent exclusions, especially if used more than sparingly. What they are reported to want above all is better peer support, not more training or theoretical guidance, and the chance to deploy professional judgement and discretion but in a context that is neither isolative nor punitive (Partridge, 2019). Consideration would be given to creating a 'practice improvement fund', as recommended by the Timpson Review but not adopted by the government, and to other new programmes, such as those proposed in 2017 by the Institute for Public Policy Research, to develop expertise in the teaching profession, connect exceptional teachers to schools for excluded children and create a community of leaders dedicated to promoting effective practices of inclusion throughout the system and thereby acting as catalysts for change (Gill et al, 2017).

Fourthly, as far as the process to be adopted in grievance mechanisms is concerned, a postliberal approach will not favour the legalistic device of a dedicated first-tier tribunal but will encourage the continued involvement of governing boards, not merely as local champions or ambassadors, but more broadly as democratic agents and of democratically constituted Independent Review Panels, with emphasis on the recruitment to both of voices from a range of civic associations. The aim will be to develop the case-conferencing capacity of multidisciplinary panels that both represent community perspectives and have the shared learning to facilitate solutions. There will be reciprocal emphasis on the participatory readiness of all parties to the grievance process, secured not merely by training and guidance but by immersion in the ethos and practices of civic participation, and in the art of complaining, from the point of recruitment. The approach of review panels will in turn be one of deliberative and mediatory consensus-building rather than legal adjudication or consumer negotiation. To facilitate such practice, steps would be taken in the spirit of civic education to establish local information and advice services, such as those available in some SEND cases, or the information and advice meetings offered in family cases as a prelude to more deliberative practice.

Fifthly, rather than a reactive and legalistic tribunal, a postliberal approach would favour final recourse to a forward-looking ombud-type institution, locally or regionally based, so it could take advantage of local knowledge and purposive intervention, including by way of own-initiative enquiry. Instead of pursuing 'modern ombudsman practice' based largely on New Public Management principles, the locally based ombud would embrace participatory, democratic and enabling practices, with an emphasis on inquisitorial intelligence gathering, deliberative problem-solving, systemic and restorative remedy, and a commitment to disseminating shared local learning.

The ambition of postliberal approaches of this sort would be active citizen participation in making real the social entitlement to education. Such entitlement is itself humanistic in its aspiration to develop and sustain human capability. The grievance mechanisms deployed would be similarly humanistic in respecting the dignity of human personhood shared by all – parents, street-level bureaucrats and teachers; pluralist in entailing the mobilization of civil society and social advocacy; and Idealist in prefacing the invocation of the enabling and ethical state – local, regional and national – as an indispensable partner. Such would be the key elements of the postliberal framework summoned in aid of this small place of reawakened democratic citizenship.

9

Conclusion

In a celebrated essay published in 1958, cultural critic Raymond Williams argued that 'culture is ordinary', by which he meant that it comprises both common meanings and special processes of discovery and creative effort (Williams, 1958). Over 60 years later, former Labour MP and Chair of the House of Commons Public Administration Select Committee, Tony Wright, alluded to Williams' essay in arguing that in a similar way democratic politics is ordinary, most conspicuously practised in the context of everyday life and common meanings (Wright, 2012). Administrative justice is ordinary justice, rooted in the everyday relationships of citizen and state and summoned in aid when those relationships break down. If its therapy is to be transformative, it must be social rather than resolutely individualistic, aimed at providing balm to wounds that are political, in the sense that they derive from the shared experience of the citizen body and entail healing that transcends the individual case. The justice inherent in public administration is the justice inherent in the common good. To realize that form of social justice, its background assumptions and ways of proceeding must be responsive to social need in ways that go beyond individual or legal justice. Administrative justice is, in other words, something more than 'administrative justice'.

The poetry of street-level bureaucracy

It is rarely that the word 'Ombudsman' appears in a published volume of poetry. Yet it does so in a poem by Irish poet Dennis O'Driscoll in his 2012 collection, *Dear Life*. O'Driscoll, apart from a career as one of contemporary Ireland's most celebrated poets and the distinction of compiling a collection of acclaimed interviews with his friend Seamus Heaney, spent almost 40 years as an official in Ireland's Revenue and Customs service. The bureaucratic provenance of aspects of his work is playfully betrayed by titles such as 'Head Office', 'Best Practice' and 'Paper Trail', even when the subject-matter is not ostensibly that of his own desk and office. In 'Revenue and Customs', we hear how at the end of a working day the computer files are backed up, the water cooler left to its own devices and the open-plan office abandoned for the night. It is then that the 'unfinished business ... is put on hold', including 'the tricky queries' and, tellingly perhaps, the 'Ombudsman appeals'. Meanwhile, every Tuesday, the Revenue Choir, whose daily clientele at the office is invariably 'rancorous', gathers for choir practice, putting a 'brave face on their way of life', in solidarity and friendship (O'Driscoll, 2012: 41–5).

Such reflections conjure an ambience familiar to the inhabitant of any modern office and hint too at something of the camaraderie that in bureaucratic routine bridges workplace diversity, harmony breaking out between 'the contralto from / Large Cases and the bass from Prosecutions' (O'Driscoll, 2012). In such moments, there come to mind former colleagues now long-dead, their daily habits and professional idiosyncrasies. These are images that disclose the human context of the street-level bureaucracies with which this book began, in all their banality, contestation, diversity and richness.

Postliberal politics seek to credit that human context of street-level bureaucracy and to find in it the dignity of human labour, the work of democratic citizenship as production rather than consumption, and of shared endeavour rather than solo mission. Reciprocal to that manifestation of citizenship is the active citizenship of those, never less than rightfully 'rancorous', who encounter in those street-level bureaucrats the shape and texture of the democratic state, and who expect to find there an image of their own diversity and connectivity. As Allen has observed: 'A connected society is one that maximizes active – in the sense of alive and engaged – bridging ties. This generally takes the work of institutions' (Allen, 2016: 88).

The offices of everyday public administration are central among those 'bridging institutions', as are the everyday institutions of administrative justice, such as public ombuds, tribunals and civic mediators, with the potential to play a decisive role in creating a connected society. In the context of postliberal politics, the sustained connectivity of such a society will worship at the altar of neither the state nor the individual, yet it will recognize the reciprocal value of both: the relational and partnership state as ethical enabler of social entitlement, the socially embedded individual as co-producer of problem-solving democratic practice. Mediating between individual and state is that myriad network of civic association, the seedbed of a culture that is constructed in common, not commonly imposed from without.

In the context of such a postliberal politics, the function of ombuds, tribunals and civic mediators is unavoidably political, in the sense that their interactions with citizens are a privileged setting for the social conversations that constitute everyday politics. The response to citizen grievance is hallowed democratic activity, not the mere satisfaction of consumer demand or user expectation. As Daniel Blake proclaimed in Ken Loach's film, his identity is that of citizen, nothing more, nothing less.

Yet if Loach's films, from *Cathy Come Home* in the mid-1960s to the contemporary narratives of *I, Daniel Blake, Sorry We Missed You*, and *The Old Oak* are excruciating exposures of the contradictions of contemporary liberal democracy, his idealization of a lost social democratic past, most notably in *The Spirit of '45* with its depiction of British wartime solidarity and subsequent achievements of the Atlee government, appears remote from the neoliberal, cosmopolitan and technological context of the 21st century. The pluralist version of postliberalism does not seek refuge in nostalgia, despite its humanistic and Idealist credentials. There is a pragmatic strain too, which celebrates reason and realism and is drawn as a result to the anchored realities of place, community and socially embedded personhood. It is in bridging ties, not the personal bonds of ascribed identity, that it seeks to build the connected society that pluralist modernity demands.

The responsive legality of postliberalism

If the foundations of contemporary liberalism have rested upon a form of legalism that privileges the court rather than the deliberative assembly as the primary model of decision-making, for postliberalism the displacement of that ascendancy is a priority. It has been suggested throughout this book that the insights of Nonet and Selznick, forged in the 1960s and 1970s, provide a still valuable jurisprudential framework for moving beyond the forms of autonomous law of which liberal legalism can be construed as a deformation. Responsive law offers an alternative that finds in the 'rule of reason' a pragmatic and problem-solving adaptability to changing social context. Responsive law transcends the restricted commandments of formalism and proceduralism and instead aspires to more affirmative, substantive and transformative engagement with citizen grievance. Its priority is not so much adjudication as civic deliberation and the restoration of trust, the translation of costly social relationships into connections of reciprocal benefit. Morris Jones' insight in the 1940s that the problem with bureaucracy is at root a problem in relationships holds good.

The idea and practice of responsive legality have a history. They are not without context and precedent. On the contrary, just as postliberalism entails the restoration of lost strands of liberal thought, so responsive legality entails the revival of aspects of legal thought that, although never entirely lost, have been obscured from view by the fog of legalism. In the public administration literature of the interwar years and in the mid-century ambitions for the public ombud, there were sown the seeds of an incipiently responsive legality that gradually succumbed to traditional legal methods and to the dogged survival of judicial forms as the default option for response to citizen grievance. Such submission, it should be noted, was notwithstanding the best intentions and ingenuity of successive generations of individual commentators and practitioners. Yet it is the hegemonic force of legalism as a social imaginary rather than its efficacy as mere technique that has so often won out, sapping the energy of alternative visions in its capacious advance.

Disability human rights, because of their provenance within the fold of liberal legalism, can be seen in this context as a jurisprudential fifth column. Working surreptitiously from a base within equality law that was expressive of rights-based legalism, adversarialism and the 'American way of law', disability human rights in theory and practice have transcended liberal legalism with responsive legality as a framework for mediating between citizen and state. As the discussion of the mental health system and the special educational needs and disability system in England has suggested, notwithstanding that paradigm shift, the allure of liberal legalism nevertheless endures, so that responsive advances are in constant tension with periodic relapse into legalistic forms and procedures.

The challenges facing liberal democracies since the financial crash of 2008 and global pandemic of 2020 have become so acute that postliberal politics reflect an already changed environment. In so doing, they provide renewed energy for responsive legality as a commensurate form of law, as an aspect of everyday politics, and as unavoidable engagement with the new paradigm inaugurated by the recognition of disability human rights.

The justice of the common good

Central to the ambitions of postliberalism is the displacement of justice as merely procedural fairness from its pre-eminence among public values. In this, postliberalism builds on the legacy of those communitarian critiques of Rawlsian liberalism that found acute expression in the 1980s and 1990s. While suspicious of communitarian forms that aspire to an exclusive mode of 'common good constitutionalism', pluralist postliberalism nevertheless seeks to situate individual rights, proceduralism and individualized forms of justice amid a richer suite of values and virtues. Just as Lorenzetti's depiction of good government made justice subordinate to the common good and placed it alongside the other cardinal virtues, so postliberalism, and the post-legalism it generates, shares Shklar's mistrust of the 'legalistic distortion of experience' and its overheated dramatization of 'stark choice and great decision' at the expense of ordinary virtue and vice. By reinstating the sovereignty of good, at the expense of the philosophy of right, postliberalism invites entry to a more complex ethical domain and to the deliberative exercise of phronesis as the chief means of navigation.

The prioritization of the good and of deliberative decision-making leads, in the context of response to citizen grievance, to the question of how in practice the goal of adjudication might be made subordinate to the purposive affirmation of social goods and public benefit. From that readjustment of priority flow the many variations of process and institutional design proposed in an administrative justice context: the creation of own-initiative powers of investigation for ombuds; the ability of ombuds and tribunals to offer restorative remedy; the practices of therapeutic justice, case-conferencing and consensus-building as forms of civic mediation that can humanize the rough edges of legal procedure. Such reforms seek to transcend the confines of 'administrative justice' as bureaucratic, professional, moralistic, managerialist or consumerist decision-making, and instead embrace values of the common good and social rights entitlement that scarcely fit the ordinary sense of individualized or legal 'justice' at all. In the search for holistic administrative justice, the ambition becomes one of escaping the iron cage not so much of bureaucracy but of Weber's other protagonist, legal rationality, displacing the artificial reason of law with the responsive practices of the law of reason.

At the same time, such initiatives return public administration and response to citizen grievance to the realm of democratic politics. Too often, responsive reform has foundered on the lack of political will, at times on the lack of political interest, the realm of public administration and administrative justice too remote from the grand places of policy to warrant much attention. Reinstated as the 'linchpins' of democratic citizenship, public authorities and street-level bureaucracy become a site of critical importance to the sustenance of the democratic state. Through the orchestration of organizational phronesis, ombuds, tribunals and civic mediators in turn exercise a privileged function in the realization of democratic citizenship, facilitating the participatory readiness of street-level bureaucrats and of aggrieved citizens alike. On the other side of the pandemic portal lies the potential consolation of a connected society, pluralist and purposeful, resolute in its valuation of social complexity and suspicion of extreme singularity. Access to its balm is through the path of everyday politics, the daily churn of public administration and the business of responding to the grievances it inevitably generates. It is a way that is humane and holistic, consensual and connected; it is a way that finds in responsive legality an instrument of democratic politics fit for a postliberal age.

Going on together

The medium of that postliberal politics is everyday democracy, the 'micropolitics' of everyday life (Wright, 2012: 79). It credits the Aristotelian insight that human beings are political animals, in the sense that their flourishing can only occur in community and that the establishment of stable community entails the daily management of difference. That process of diversity-management is not the business exclusively, or even primarily, of politicians; nor can whole spheres of human activity, such as dispute-resolution and response to grievance, be cordoned off from politics.

It would be a mistake to think that daily decisions about the allocation of social goods and the resources that go into them are somehow immunized from contagion with politics, that procedural hygiene forms an effective prophylactic against the messiness of conflicting interest. Equally, 'the common good' cannot provide secure refuge if it is taken to denote the existence, prior to political contestation, of an overlapping consensus, still less the imposition of enforced unison. Instead, the common good is the process of reconciling diverse interests, of achieving together a form of consensus rather than acquiescing in the ascription of uniformity.

The way in which diverse groups cohere is not through prior agreement about fundamentals but through the practice of politics. The response to citizen grievance through the practice of 'administrative justice' is not to be seen as an activity that approximates to legal adjudication but rather as a paradigmatic expression of political agency. The defence of responsive legality as the template of postliberal administrative justice is in other words an aspect of the larger ambition of 'the defence of politics' (Crick, 1962).

The corridors of administrative power, like those haunted in O'Driscoll's Revenue and Customs office, do not glitter in the spotlight of public affection or media interest. They lack the glamour and panache of parliamentary skirmish and the majesty and solemnity of the law. Yet they are the places where the 'fragile moral economy' of democratic life persists, as ordinary citizens go on together with the business of their everyday lives (Zacka, 2017).

The practice of 'going on together' under 'always imperfect conditions of democracy and justice' is to be valued 'in much the same way we value the more familiar political goods of liberty and equality' (Ober, 2005: 2). With the benefit of having chaired the then Public Administration Select Committee, Wright, reflecting on the civic tradition, has observed that '[i]t is in the nature of citizenship that it has to be regularly practised if it is to be kept in good condition. Inactivity soon produces atrophy' (Wright, 2012: 58). The challenge is to explore ways in which democratic participation can be enlarged and the 'culture of citizenship nourished': the uninviting alternative is 'to leave the activity of politics to a professional political class and to settle for the role of subject-consumer' (Wright, 2012: 58).

When the business of going on together fractures in the face of citizen grievance, the task of putting the pieces back together, often in a new form, falls to those within, and without, public administration charged with the task of responding to those grievances and of doing so by exercising the virtue of administrative justice. As the coalition of postliberal politics and responsive legality insists, it is a virtue whose practice on the other side of the pandemic portal entails once more its emancipation from the straitjacket of liberal legalism. It is a virtue moreover whose practice is 'everyday', the stuff of small places, devoid of posture and ceremony, of arcane rites, rules and techniques: like culture and politics, administrative justice is ordinary, and its ordinariness, like theirs, is that of the street.

References

Abraham, A. (2009) 'The Ombudsman and the constitution', Gabrielle Ganz Lecture, Southampton University, 22 October 2009 [unpublished].

Adler, M. (2003) 'A socio-legal approach to administrative justice', *Law and Policy*, 25(4): 323–52.

Adler, M. (2006) 'Fairness in context', *Journal of Law and Society*, 33(4): 615–38.

Adler, M. (ed) (2010a) *Administrative Justice in Context*, Oxford: Hart.

Adler, M. (2010b) 'Social security and social welfare', in P. Cane and H.M. Kritzer (eds) *The Oxford Handbook of Empirical Legal Research*, Oxford: Oxford University Press, pp 399–23.

Adler, M. (2018) *Cruel, Inhuman or Degrading Treatment: Benefit Sanctions in the UK*, London: Palgrave Pivot.

Allen, D. (2016) *Education and Equality*, Chicago: University of Chicago Press.

Anderson, P. (2021) 'Ever closer union?', *London Review of Books*, 43(1): 25–34.

Ansell, C. (2011) *Pragmatist Democracy: Evolutionary Learning as Public Philosophy*, Oxford: Oxford University Press.

Baiocchi, G. (2003) 'Participation, activism and politics: the Porto Alegre experiment', in A. Fung and E.O. Wright (eds) *Deepening Democracy: Institutional Innovations in Empowered Governance*, London: Verso, pp 45–76.

Bagenstos, S. (2004) 'The future of disability law', *Yale Law Journal*, 114(1): 10–83.

Bagenstos, S. (2009) *Law and the Contradictions of the Disability Rights Movement*, New Haven: Yale.

Baggini, J. (2008) *Complaint: From Minor Moans to Principled Protests*, London: Profile Books.

Ball, S. (ed) (2015) *Defending Politics: Bernard Crick at the Political Quarterly*, Oxford: Political Quarterly Publishing Company.

Barker, E. (1906) *The Political Thought of Plato and Aristotle*, London: G.P. Putnam & Sons.

Barker, R. (1978) *Political Ideas in Modern Britain*, London: Methuen & Co.

Beaupart, F., Carney, T., Chiarella, M., Satchell, C., Walton, M., Bennett, B. et al (2014) 'Regulating healthcare complaints: a literature review', *International Journal of Health Care Quality Assurance*, 27(6): 505–18.

Ben Jelloun, T. (2016) *By Fire: Writings on the Arab Spring*, trans R.S. Nezami, Evanston, IL: Northwestern University Press.

Bentley, T. (2005) *Everyday Democracy*, London: Demos.

Bhuwania, A. (2017) *Courting the People: Public Interest Litigation in Post-Emergency India*, Cambridge: Cambridge University Press.

Blunkett, The Rt Hon Lord (2019) 'Foreword', in Sir B. Massie, *A Life without Limits*, Cirencester: Mereo Books.

Bondy, V. and Doyle, M. (2018) 'What's in a name? A discussion paper on ombud terminology', in M. Hertogh and R. Kirkham (eds) *Research Handbook on the Ombudsman*, Cheltenham: Edward Elgar Publishing, pp 485–506.

Box, M. (1983) *Rebel Advocate: A Biography of Gerald Gardiner*, London: Victor Gollancz.

Boyle, N. (1997) *Who Are We Now? Christian Humanism and the Global Market from Hegel to Heaney*, Notre Dame: University of Notre Dame Press.

Boyson, S. (2020) 'Mediation in French administrative courts: what lessons for administrative justice?', *Northern Ireland Legal Quarterly*, 71(3): 457–79.

Brodkin, E. (2017) 'The ethnographic turn in political science: reflections on the state of the art', *Political Science and Politics*, 50(1): 131–4.

Brown, M. and Jones, R. (2021) *Paint Your Town Red: How Preston Took Back Control and Your Town Can Too*, London: Repeater Books.

Brown, W. and Halley, J. (eds) (2002a) *Left Legalism/Left Critique*, Durham and London: Duke University Press.

Brown, W. and Halley, J. (2002b) 'Introduction', in W. Brown and J. Halley (eds) *Left Legalism/Left Critique*, Durham and London: Duke University Press, pp 1–36.

Buck, T., Kirkham, R. and Thompson, B. (2011) *The Ombudsman Enterprise and Administrative Justice*, Farnham: Ashgate.

Buddery, P., Parsfield, M. and Shafique, A. (2016) *Changing the Narrative*, London: Royal Society of Arts.

Burrow, J. (2000) *The Crisis of Reason: European Thought, 1848–1914*, New Haven: Yale University Press.

Bynoe, I., Oliver, M. and Barnes, C. (1991) *Equal Rights for Disabled People: The Case for a New Law*, London: IPPR.

Cane, P. and Kritzer, H.M. (eds) (2010). *The Oxford Handbook of Empirical Legal Research*, Oxford: Oxford University Press.

Care Quality Commission (2017) 'The state of care in mental health services 2014 to 2017', London: The Stationery Office.

Care Quality Commission (2022) 'Monitoring the Mental Health Act in 2020/21', London: The Stationery Office.

Carney, T. (2010) 'Involuntary mental health treatment laws: the "rights" and "wrongs" of competing models', in B. McSherry and P. Weller (eds) *Rethinking Rights-Based Mental Health Laws*, Oxford: Hart, pp 257–74.

Carney, T. (2011) 'Mental health tribunals as governance: lessons from an Australian study', Sydney Law School, Legal Studies Research Paper no 11/12, February 2011.

Carver, R. (2018) *A Mission for Justice: The International Ombudsman Institute 1978–2018*, Vienna: Verlag Osterreich GmbH.

Chamot, M., Farr, D. and Butlin, M. (1964) *The Modern British Paintings, Drawings and Sculpture*, vol 1, London: Oldbourne Press.

Choudhry, S., Khosla, M. and Mehta, P. (eds) (2016) *The Oxford Handbook of the Indian Constitution*, New Delhi: Oxford University Press.

Clements, L. (2020) *Clustered Injustice and the Level Green*, London: Legal Action Group.

Cocks, R. (2014) 'Sustaining the character of a judge: conflict within the legal thought of British India', *Journal of Legal History*, 35(1): 44–67.

Cole, G.D.H. (1913) *The World of Labour*, London: G. Bell and Son.

Committee on the Rights of Persons with Disabilities (2018) 'General Comment No 6 on Equality and Non-Discrimination', Adopted at 19th session 14 February–9 March 2018.

Cottam, H. (2018) *Radical Help: How We Can Remake the Relationships between Us and Revolutionise the Welfare State*, London: Virago.

Creutzfeldt, N. (2018) *Ombudsmen and ADR: A Comparative Study of Informal Justice in Europe*, Cham, Switzerland: Springer and Palgrave Macmillan.

Creutzfeldt, N. (2020) 'Managing complaints: focusing on users and non-users of the system', in R. Kirkham and C. Gill (eds) *A Manifesto for Ombudsman Reform*, Cham, Switzerland: Palgrave Macmillan, pp 109–126.

Creutzfeldt, N., Gill, C., Cornelis, M. and McPherson, R. (2021) *Access to Justice for Vulnerable and Energy-Poor Consumers: Just Energy?*, Oxford: Hart.

Crick, B. (1962) *In Defence of Politics*, London: Weidenfeld & Nicolson.

Crick, B. (1965) 'The prospects for parliamentary reform', *Political Quarterly*, 36(3): 333–46; reprinted in Ball, S. (2015), pp 95–106.

Cruddas, J. (2021) *The Dignity of Labour*, Cambridge: Polity.

Davar, B. (2015) 'Disabilities, colonisation and globalisation: how the very possibility of a disability identity was compromised for the "insane" in India', in H. Spandler, J. Anderson and B. Sapey (eds) *Madness, Distress and the Politics of Disablement*, Bristol: Policy Press, pp 215–27.

De Beco, G. (ed) (2013) *Article 33 of the UN Convention on the Rights of Persons with Disabilities: National Structures for the Implementation and Monitoring of the Convention*, Leiden: Martinus Nijhoff.

De Certeau, M. (1984) *The Practice of Everyday Life*, Berkeley: University of California Press.

De Langen, M., Govers, E. and van Zutphen, R. (2018) 'Effectiveness and independence of the ombudsman's own-motion investigations: a practitioner's perspective from the Netherlands', in M. Hertogh and R. Kirkham (eds) *Research Handbook on the Ombudsman*, Cheltenham: Edward Elgar Publishing, pp 373–92.

Degener, T. (2017) 'A new human rights model of disability', in V. Della Fina, R. Cera and G. Palmsiano (eds) *The United Nations Convention on the Rights of Persons with Disabilities*, Cham: Springer, pp 41–59.

Della Fina, V., Cera, R., and Palmisano, G. (eds) (2017) *The United Nations Convention on the Rights of Persons with Disabilities*, Cham: Springer.

Department for Education (2022) 'Suspension and permanent exclusion from maintained schools, academies and pupil referral units in England, including pupil movement: guidance for maintained schools, academies, and pupil referral units in England', London: The Stationery Office.

Dewey, J. (1916) *Democracy and Education*, New York: Macmillan.

Dewey, J. (1976–88) *The Middle Works*, Carbondale: Southern Illinois University Press.

Diez, L. (2018) 'The use of own-initiative powers by the ombudsman', in M. Hertogh and R. Kirkham (eds) *Research Handbook on the Ombudsman*, Cheltenham: Edward Elgar Publishing, pp 354–72.

Disability Rights Commission (2002) 'Code of practice on rights of access, goods, facilities, services and premises', London: The Stationery Office.

Disability Rights Commission (2007) 'DRC legal achievements 2000–2007', London: DRC.

Divan, S. (2016), 'Public interest litigation', in S. Choudhry, M. Khosla and P. Mehta (eds) *The Oxford Handbook of the Indian Constitution*, New Delhi: Oxford University Press, pp 662–79.

Dodds, E. (1936) *Humanism and Technique in Greek Studies*, Oxford: Clarendon Press.

Donnelly, M. (2010) 'Reviews of treatment decisions: legalism, process and the protection of rights', in B. McSherry and P. Weller (eds) *Rethinking Rights-Based Mental Health Laws*, Oxford: Hart, pp 275–98.

Douglas, M. (1987) *How Institutions Think*, London: Routledge.

Doyle, M. (2007) 'Enforcing rights through mediation', in Disability Rights Commission, 'DRC legal achievements 2000–2007', London: DRC, pp 57–64.

Doyle, M. (2019) 'A place at the table: a report on young people's participation in resolving disputes about special educational needs and disabilities', Colchester: UKAJI.

Doyle, M. (2022) 'What the SEND Green Paper tells us about the state of administrative justice', UKAJI blog, 7 July, Available from: www.essexc aji.org/2022/07/

Doyle, M. and O'Brien, N. (2019) *Reimagining Administrative Justice: Human Rights in Small Places*, Cham, Switzerland: Springer and Palgrave Macmillan.

Drewry, G. (2009) 'The judicialisation of "administrative" tribunals in the UK: from Hewart to Legatt', *Transylvanian Review of Administrative Sciences*, 5(28): 45–64.

Dubois, V. (2016) *The Bureaucrat and the Poor: Encounters in French Welfare Offices*, trans J.-Y. Bart, London: Routledge.

Dunleavy, P., Loughlin, M., Margetts, H., Bastow, S., Tinkler, J., Pearce, O. et al (2005) 'Citizen redress: what citizens can do if things go wrong with public services', National Audit Office Value for Money Report, HC 529, London: The Stationery Office.

Dunleavy, P., Bastow, S., Tinkler, J., Goldchluck, S. and Towers, E. (2010) 'Joining up citizen redress in UK central government', in M. Adler (ed) *Administrative Justice in Context*, Oxford: Hart, pp 421–56.

Eagleton, T. (1967) 'The idea of a common culture', in S. Regan (ed) *The Eagleton Reader*, Oxford: Blackwell, pp 104–16.

Eagleton, T. (1994) 'The right and the good: postmodernism and the liberal state', in S. Regan (ed) *The Eagleton Reader*, Oxford: Blackwell, pp 294–303.

Education Committee (2022) 'Oral evidence', 24 May, the government's SEND Review, HC 235.

Equality and Human Rights Commission (2022) 'Response to the Mental Health Bill 2022', London: EHRC.

Fassin, D. (2015) *At the Heart of the State: The Moral World of Institutions*, London: Pluto Press.

Ferguson, L. (2021) 'Vulnerable children's right to education, school exclusion, and pandemic law-making', *Emotional and Behavioural Difficulties*, 26(1): 101–15.

Fletcher, A. and O'Brien, N. (2008) 'Disability Rights Commission: from civil rights to social rights', *Journal of Law and Society*, 35(4): 520–50.

Forrester, K. (2019) *In the Shadow of Justice: Postwar Liberalism and the Remaking of Political Philosophy*, Princeton: Princeton University Press.

Foster, S. and Iaione, C. (2016) 'The city as a commons', *Yale Law and Policy Review*, 34(2): 281–349.

Fredman, S. (2008) *Human Rights Transformed: Positive Rights and Positive Duties*, Oxford: Oxford University Press.

Fredman, S., Kuosmanen, J. and Campbell, M. (2016) 'Transformative equality: making sustainable development goals work for women', *Ethics and International Affairs*, 30(2): 177–87.

Fukuyama, F. (2022) *Liberalism and Its Discontents*, London: Profile Books.

Fung, A. and Wright, E.O. (2003) *Deepening Democracy: Institutional Innovations in Empowered Governance*, London: Verso.

Ganguly, A. (2015) *Landmark Judgments that Changed India*, New Delhi: Rupa Publications.

Gearty, C. (2016) *On Fantasy Island: Britain, Europe and Human Rights*, Oxford: Oxford University Press.

Gearty, C. and Douzinas, C. (eds) (2012) *The Cambridge Companion to Human Rights Law*, Cambridge: Cambridge University Press.

Gill, C. (2020a) 'The ombud and "Complaint Standards Authority" powers', in R. Kirkham and C. Gill (eds) *A Manifesto for Ombudsman Reform*, Cham, Switzerland: Palgrave Macmillan, pp 95–107.

Gill, C. (2020b) 'The ombud and own-initiative investigation powers', in R. Kirkham and C. Gill (eds) *A Manifesto for Ombudsman Reform*, Cham, Switzerland: Palgrave Macmillan, pp 77–94.

Gill, C., Sapouna, M., Hirst, C. and Williams, J. (2019) 'Dysfunctional accountability in complaint systems: the effects of complaints on public service employees', *Public Law (October)*, 644–64.

Gill, C., Mullen, T. and Vivian, N. (2020) 'The managerial ombudsman', *Modern Law Review*, 83(4): 797–830.

Gill, K., Quilter-Pinner, H. and Swift, D. (2017) 'Making the difference: breaking the link between school exclusion and social exclusion', London: IPPR.

Glover-Thomas, N. (2002) *Reconstructing Mental Health Law and Policy*, London: Butterworths.

Goluboff, R. (2013) 'Lawyers, Law and the new civil rights history', *Harvard Law Review*, 126(8): 2312–35.

Gooding, C. (1994) *Disabling Laws, Disabling Acts: Disability Rights in Britain and America*, London: Pluto Press.

Gostin, L. (1983) 'Contemporary historical perspectives on mental health reform', *Journal of Law and Society*, 10(1): 47–70.

Gostin, L. (2007) 'From a civil libertarian to a sanitarian', *Journal of Law and Society*, 34(4): 594–616.

Gray, J. (1993) *Post-Liberalism: Studies in Political Thought*, London: Routledge.

Gray, J. (2000) *Two Faces of Liberalism*, Cambridge: Polity.

Green, T.H. (1895) *Lectures on the Principles of Political Obligation*, Oxford: Clarendon Press.

Griffith, J. (1977) *The Politics of the Judiciary*, London: Fontana.

Groves, M. and Stuhmcke, A. (eds) (2022) *The Ombudsman in the Modern State*, Oxford: Hart.

Guinier, L. (2013) 'Courting the people: demosprudence and the law/politics divide', *Harvard Law Review*, 127(1): 37–44.

Guinier, L. and Torres, G. (2014) 'Changing the wind: notes towards a demosprudence of law and social movements', *Yale Law Journal*, 123(8): 2742–804.

Gulland, J. (2022) 'Social justice and administrative justice', in M. Hertogh, R. Kirkham, R. Thomas and J. Tomlinson (eds) *The Oxford Handbook of Administrative Justice*, Oxford: Oxford University Press, pp 245–62.

Gwyn, W. (1971) 'The Labour Party and the threat of bureaucracy', *Political Studies*, 19(4): 383–402.

Hall, D., Kaye, S. and Morgan, C. (2021) 'How the pandemic has accelerated the shift towards participatory public authorities', in G. Smith and T. Hughes (eds) *Democracy in a Pandemic: Participation in Response to Crisis*, London: University of Westminster Press, pp 139–53.

Halliday, S. and Scott, C. (2010) 'A cultural analysis of administrative justice', in M. Adler (ed) *Administrative Justice in Context*, Oxford: Hart, pp 183–202.

Hankins, J. (2019) *Virtue Politics: Soulcraft and Statecraft in Renaissance Italy*, Cambridge, MA: The Belknap Press of Harvard University Press.

Harlow, C. (1978) 'Ombudsmen in search of a role', *Modern Law Review*, 41(4): 446–54.

Harlow, C. (2018) 'Ombudsmen: "hunting lions" or "swatting flies"', in M. Hertogh and R. Kirkham (eds) *Research Handbook on the Ombudsman*, Cheltenham: Edward Elgar Publishing, pp 73–89.

Harlow, C. and Rawlings, R. (2009) *Law and Administration* (3rd edn), London: Butterworths.

Harris, N. and Riddell, S. (eds) (2011) *Resolving Disputes about Educational Provision: A Comparative Perspective on Special Educational Needs*, Farnham: Ashgate.

Harris, N. (2011) 'Dispute resolution in education roles and models', in N. Harris and S. Riddell (eds) *Resolving Disputes about Educational Provision: A Comparative Perspective on Special Educational Needs*, Farnham: Ashgate, pp 25–48.

Harris, N. and Smith, E. (2011) 'On the right track? The resolution of special educational needs disputes in England', in N. Harris and S. Riddell (eds) *Resolving Disputes about Educational Provision: A Comparative Perspective on Special Educational Needs*, Farnham: Ashgate, pp 49–102.

Health Select Committee (2009) 'Patient safety', HC 151, London: The Stationery Office.

Henshaw, P. (2021), 'SEND: Ofsted report tackles co-production, SENCOs, and EHCP delays', in *SecEd Bulletin* 19 May 2021, Available from: https://sec-ed.co.uk/news/send-ofsted-report-tackles-co-production-sencos-and-ehcp-delays-families-inclusion/

Hepple, B. (2011) *Equality: The New Legal Framework*, Oxford: Hart.

Hepple, B., Coussey, M. and Choudhury, T. (2000) *Equality: A New Framework. Report of the Independent Review on the Enforcement of UK Anti-Discrimination Legislation*, Oxford: Hart.

Hertogh, M. (2010) 'Through the eyes of bureaucrats: how frontline officials understand administrative justice', in M. Adler (ed) *Administrative Justice in Context*, Oxford: Hart, pp 203–25.

Hertogh, M. (2018) *Nobody's Law: Legal Consciousness and Legal Alienation in Everyday Life*, London: Palgrave Macmillan.

Hertogh, M. and Kirkham, R. (eds) (2018) *Research Handbook on the Ombudsman*, Cheltenham: Edward Elgar Publishing.

Hertogh, M., Kirkham, R., Thomas, R. and Tomlinson, J. (eds) (2022) *The Oxford Handbook of Administrative Justice*, Oxford: Oxford University Press.

Hirschl, R. (2004) *Towards Juristocracy: The Origins and Consequences of the New Constitutionalism*, Cambridge, MA: Harvard University Press.

Hodgkinson, A. and Vickerman, P. (2009) *Key Issues in Special Educational Needs and Inclusion*, London: Sage.

Hospital for Mental Health, Ahmedabad (2013) 'Towards excellence in mental health: celebrating 150 years of journey', Ahmedabad: Hospital for Mental Health, Ahmedabad.

Hughes, R. (1993) *Culture of Complaint*, New York: Warner Books.

Hunter, R. and Leonard, A. (1997) 'Sex discrimination and alternative dispute resolution: British proposals in the light of international experience', (Summer) *Public Law*, (Summer): 293–314.

Hupe, P., Hill, M. and Buffat, A. (2016) 'Introduction: defining and understanding street-level bureaucracy', in P. Hupe, M. Hill and A. Buffat (eds) *Understanding Street-Level Bureaucracy*. Bristol: Policy Press, pp 3–24.

Hupe, P., Hill, M. and Buffat, A. (eds) (2016) *Understanding Street-Level Bureaucracy*, Bristol: Policy Press.

Hurwitz, S. (1960) 'The Danish Ombudsman and his Office' (1624) *The Listener*, 12 May, 835–38.

Hutchinson, A. and Monahan, P. (eds) (1987) *The Rule of Law: Ideal or Ideology*, Toronto: Carswell.

Iaione, C. and Cannavo, P. (2015), 'The collaborative and polycentric governance of the urban and local commons', *Urban Pampleteer#5*, 29–31. Available from: www.urbanpamphleteer.org/global-education-for-urban-futures

Independent Mental Health Taskforce (2016) 'The five year forward view for mental health', London: The Stationery Office.

International Ombudsman Institute (2012) 'Wellington Declaration', Vienna: IOI.

Jones, K. (1993) *Asylums and After: A Revised History of the Mental Health Services from the Early 18th Century to the 1990s*, London: Athlone Press.

Justice (2019) 'Challenging school exclusions', London: Justice.

Kagan, R. (2001) *Adversarial Legalism: The American Way of Law*, Cambridge, MA: Harvard University Press.

Kelemen, R. (2011) *Eurolegalism: The Transformation of Law and Regulation in the European Union*, Cambridge, MA: Harvard University Press.

Kelemen, R. and Vanhala, L. (2010) 'The shift to the rights model of disability in the EU and Canada', *Regional and Federal Studies*, 20(1): 1–18.

Kirkham, R. (2022) 'The ombud as a chameleon: a study of adaptation to different administrative cultures', in M. Hertogh, R. Kirkham, R. Thomas and J. Tomlinson (eds) *The Oxford Handbook of Administrative Justice*, Oxford: Oxford University Press, pp 89–114.

Kirkham, R. and Gill, C. (eds) (2020) *A Manifesto for Ombudsman Reform*, Cham, Switzerland: Palgrave Macmillan.

Kristeva, J. (2010) *Hatred and Forgiveness*, trans J. Herman, New York: Columbia University Press.

Labour Party (1964) 'The new Britain', London: Labour Party.

Lacey, S. (2011) *Cathy Come Home*, Basingstoke: Palgrave Macmillan.

Lamb, Sir B. (2009) 'Lamb Inquiry: special educational needs and parental confidence', London: The Stationery Office.

Laverty, P. and Loach, K. (2016) *I, Daniel Blake*, Pontefract: Route Publishing.

Lawson, A. (2018) 'Uses of the Convention on the Rights of Persons with Disabilities in domestic courts', in A. Lawson and L. Waddington (eds) *The UN Convention on the Rights of Persons with Disabilities in Practice: A Comparative Analysis of the Role of Courts*, Oxford: Oxford University Press, pp 556–75.

Lawson, A. and Waddington, L. (eds) (2018) *The UN Convention on the Rights of Persons with Disabilities in Practice: A Comparative Analysis of the Role of Courts*, Oxford: Oxford University Press.

Lawson, M. (2022) 'Disabled by a real Catch-22: rage against the bureaucracy machine', *The Tablet*, 3 September, 22.

Leggatt, Sir A. (2001) 'Tribunals for users: one system, one service', London: The Stationery Office.

Leigh, J. (2002) *The Cinema of Ken Loach: Art in the Service of the People*, London: Wallflower Press.

LGSCO (2017) 'Education, health and care plans: our first 100 investigations', London: The Stationery Office.

LGSCO (2019) 'Not going to plan? Education, health and care plans two years on', London: The Stationery Office.

LGSCO and PHSO (2022) 'Section 117 aftercare: guidance for practitioners', London: The Stationery Office.

Lipsky, M. (1980) *Street-Level Bureaucracy: Dilemmas of the Individual in Public Services*, New York: Russell Sage Foundation.

Longo, M. and Zacka, B. (2019) 'Political theory in an ethnographic key', *American Political Science Review*, 113(4): 1066–70.

Loughlin, M. (1992) *Public Law and Political Theory*, Oxford: Clarendon Press.

Loughlin, M. (2000) *Sword and Scales: An Examination of the Relationship between Law and Politics*, Oxford: Hart.

Loughlin, M. (2005) 'The functionalist style in public law', *University of Toronto Law Journal*, 55(3): 361–403.

Loughlin, M. (2018) 'The apotheosis of the rule of law', *Political Quarterly*, 89(4): 659–66.

Loughlin, M. (2019) 'The political constitution revisited', *King's Law Journal*, 30(1): 5–20.

Loughlin, M. (2022) *Against Constitutionalism*, Cambridge, MA: Harvard University Press.

MacIntyre, A. (1981) *After Virtue: A Study in Moral Theory*, London: Duckworth.

MacIntyre, A. (1999) *Dependent Rational Animals: Why Human Beings Need the Virtues*, London: Duckworth.

Mackenzie, N. (ed) (1958) *Conviction*, London: MacGibbon and Kee.

Mackenzie, P. (2021) 'Making democracy work', London: Demos.

Manzini, E. (2019) *Politics of the Everyday*, London: Bloomsbury.

Martinez, J. (2022) *All of Us*, London: Nick Hern Books.

Mashaw, J. (1983) *Bureaucratic Justice: Managing Social Security Disability Claims*, New Haven: Yale University Press.

Massie, Sir B. (2019) *A Life without Limits*, Cirencester: Mereo Books.

Maynard-Moony, S. (2016) 'Foreword', in V. Dubois, *The Bureaucrat and the Poor: Encounters in French Welfare Offices*, trans J.-Y. Bart, London: Routledge, ix–xii.

Maynard-Moony, S. and Musheno, M. (2003) *Cops, Teachers, Counsellors: Stories from the Front Lines of Public Service*, Ann Arbor: University of Michigan Press.

Mazower, M. (2009) *No Enchanted Palace: The End of Empire and the Ideological Origins of the United Nations*, Princeton: Princeton University Press.

McBurnie, G. (2022) 'Understanding the response from health organisations to Health Ombudsman investigations: a new conceptual model', in M. Groves and A. Stuhmcke (eds) *The Ombudsman in the Modern State*, Oxford: Hart, pp 63–88.

McColgan, A. (2000) *Discrimination Law*, Oxford: Hart.

McCrudden, C. (2007) 'Equality legislation and reflexive regulation: a response to the discrimination law review's consultative paper', *Industrial Law Journal*, 36(3): 255–66.

McEwan, I. (2014) *The Children Act*, London: Vintage.

McSherry, B. and Weller, P. (eds) (2010) *Rethinking Rights-Based Mental Health Laws*, Oxford: Hart.

Menkel-Meadow, C. (2004/5) 'The lawyer's role(s) in deliberative democracy', *Nevada Law Journal*, 5(2): 347–69.

Menkel-Meadow, C. (2006) 'Deliberative democracy and conflict resolution: two theories and practices of participation in the polity', *Dispute Resolution Magazine*, Winter, 18–22.

Menkel-Meadow, C. (2011) 'Scaling up deliberative democracy as dispute resolution in healthcare reform: a work in progress', *Law and Contemporary Problems*, 74(1): 1–30.

Mental Health Act 1987 (India), No 14. of 1987 (22 May 1987).

Miller, P. (2001) 'A just alternative or just an alternative? Mediation and the ADA', *Ohio State Law Journal*, 62(1): 11–29.

Monaghan, K. (2007) 'Achieving strategic change through formal investigations', in Disability Rights Commission (2007) 'DRC legal achievements 2000–2007', London: DRC, pp 47–53.

Morgan, B. and Yeung, K. (2007) *An Introduction to Law and Regulation: Text and Materials*, Cambridge: Cambridge University Press.

Morris Jones, W. (1949) *Socialism and Bureaucracy*, London: Fabian Society.

Mouffe, C. (1993) *The Return of the Political*, London: Verso.

Moyn, S. (2010) *The Last Utopia: Human Rights in History*, Cambridge, MA: Harvard University Press.

Moyn, S. (2018) *Not Enough: Human Rights in an Unequal World*, Cambridge, MA: Harvard University Press.

Munro, E. (2011) 'The Munro review of child protection (final report): a child-centred system', London: The Stationery Office.

Murray, O. (1990) 'Cities of reason', in O. Murray and S. Price (eds) *The Greek City from Homer to Alexander*, Oxford: Oxford University Press, pp 1–25.

Murray, O. and Price, S. (eds) (1990) *The Greek City from Homer to Alexander*, Oxford: Oxford University Press.

Nason, S. (2016) *Reconstructing Judicial Review*, Oxford: Hart.

Nason, S. (2019) 'The "new administrative law" in Wales', *Public Law*, 703–23.

Nason, S., Sherlock, A., Pritchard, H. and Taylor, H. (2020) 'Public administration and a just Wales', Bangor and London: Bangor University and Nuffield Foundation.

Nonet, P. (1969) *Administrative Justice: Advocacy and Change in Government Agencies*, New York: Russell Sage Foundation.

Nonet, P. and Selznick, P. (2001) *Toward Responsive Law: Law and Society in Transition*, New York: Harper Torch.

Nussbaum, M. (2004) *Hiding from Humanity: Disgust, Shame, and the Law*, Princeton: Princeton University Press.

Nussbaum, M. (2006) *Frontiers of Justice: Disability, Nationality, Species Membership*, Cambridge, MA: Harvard University Press.

Nussbaum, M. (2011) *Creating Capabilities: The Human Development Approach*, Cambridge, MA: Harvard University Press.

Ober, J. (2005) *Athenian Legacies: Essays on the Politics of Going on Together*, Princeton: Princeton University Press.

O'Brien, N. (2011) 'Law and "the good life": learning disability, equality and healthcare in the UK', *The Equal Rights Review*, 6: 83–98.

O'Brien, N. (2013) 'Social rights and civil society: "Giving Force" without "Enforcement"', *Journal of Social Welfare and Family Law*, 34(4): 459–70.

O'Brien, N. (2016) 'Disability discrimination law in the United Kingdom and the new civil rights history: the contribution of Caroline Gooding', *Journal of Law and Society*, 43(3): 444–68.

O'Brien, N. (2018) 'Administrative justice in the wake of "I, Daniel Blake"', *Political Quarterly*, 89(1): 82–91.

O'Brien, N. (2020) 'The public service ombud and the claims of democracy', in R. Kirkham and C. Gill (eds) *A Manifesto for Ombudsman Reform*, Cham, Switzerland: Palgrave Macmillan, pp 41–57.

O'Brien, N. (2021) 'From "judicial mind" to "democratic soul": law and politics on the bureaucratic frontline', *Political Quarterly*, 92(1): 40–7.

O'Brien, N. (2022) 'Reimagining the classical ombud: disability rights, democracy and demosprudence', in M. Groves and A. Stuhmcke (eds) *The Ombudsman in the Modern State*, Oxford: Hart, pp 307–29.

O'Brien, N. and Thompson, B. (2010) 'Human rights and accountability in the UK: deliberative democracy and the role of the ombudsman', *European Human Rights Review*, 5: 504–12.

O'Driscoll, D. (2012) *Dear Life*, London: Anvil Press Poetry.

Ofsted (2021) 'Supporting SEND: how children and young people's special educational needs are met in mainstream schools', London: The Stationery Office.

O'Hara, G. (2011) 'Parties, people and parliament: Britain's "Ombudsman" and the politics of the 1960s', *Journal of British Studies*, 50(3): 690–714.

O'Hara, G. (2012) *Governing Post-War Britain: The Paradoxes of Progress*, Houndmills, Basingstoke: Palgrave Macmillan.

O'Neill, The Rt Hon Baroness (2018) *A Question of Trust: The BBC Reith Lectures 2002*, Cambridge: Cambridge University Press.

Orwell, G. (1941) *The Lion and the Unicorn: Socialism and the English Genius*, London: Searchlight Books.

Ostrom, E. (2012) *The Future of the Commons: Beyond Market Failure and Government Regulation*, London: The Institute of Economic Affairs.

Pabst, A. (2019) *The Demons of Liberal Democracy*, Cambridge: Polity.

Pabst, A. (2021) *Postliberal Politics*, Cambridge: Polity.

Palmer, E. (2007) *Judicial Review, Socio-Economic Rights and the Human Rights Act*, Oxford: Hart.

Paquet, G. (2009) *Scheming Virtuously: The Road to Collaborative Governance*, Ottawa: Invenire Books.

Partridge, L. (2019) 'Teachers want help to prevent school exclusions', RSA blog, 25 September, Available from: https://www.thersa.org/blog/2019/09/teacher-survey

Pathare, S., Funk, M., Bold, N.D., Chauhan, A., Kalha, J., Krishnamoorthy, S. et al (2019) 'Systematic evaluation of the QualityRights programme in public mental health facilities in Gujarat, India', *British Journal of Psychiatry*, 218(4): 1–8.

PHSO (2018) 'Maintaining momentum: driving improvements in mental health care', HC 906, London: The Stationery Office.

Pound, R. (1908) 'Liberty of contract', *Yale Law Journal*, 18(7): 454–87.

Public Administration Select Committee (PASC) (2014) 'More complaints please! Twelfth report of session 2013–14', HCC 229, London: The Stationery Office.

Putnam, R. (2000) *Bowling Alone: The Collapse and Revival of American Community*, New York: Simon & Schuster.

Quinn, G. (2012) 'Restoring the "human" in "human rights": personhood and doctrinal innovation in the UN Disability Convention', in C. Gearty and C. Douzinas (eds) *The Cambridge Companion to Human Rights Law*, Cambridge: Cambridge University Press, pp 36–55.

Quinn, G. (2013) 'Foreword', in G. de Beco (ed) *Article 33 of the UN Convention on the Rights of Persons with Disabilities: National Structures for the Implementation and Monitoring of the Convention*, Leiden: Martinus Nijhoff, pp vii–viii.

Race Relations Board (1966–7) 'Annual report 1966–67', London: The Stationery Office.

Regan, S. (ed) (1998) *The Eagleton Reader*, Oxford: Blackwell.

Resnik, J. and Curtis, D.E. (2007) 'Representing justice: from Renaissance iconography to twenty-first-century courthouses', *Proceedings of the American Philosophical Society*, 151(2): 139–83.

Resnik, J. and Curtis, D.E. (2011) *Representing Justice: Invention, Controversy, and Rights in City-States and Democratic Courtrooms*, New Haven: Yale University Press.

Restakis, J. (2022) *Civilizing the State: Reclaiming Politics for the Common Good*, Gabriola Island: New Society Publishers.

Richards, Z. (2019) *Responsive Legality: The New Administrative Justice*, Abingdon and New York: Routledge.

Richter, M. (1964) *The Politics of Conscience: T.H. Green and His Age*, New York: University Press of America.

Robson, W. (1928) *Justice and Administrative Law: A Study of the British Constitution*, London: Macmillan and Co.

Robson, W. (1932) 'The report of the Committee on Ministers' Powers', *Political Quarterly*, 3(3): 346–64.

Routledge, M. (2020) 'Commissioning for a better future: a starter for ten', London: Social Care Innovation Network.

Roy, A. (2020) *Azadi: Freedom, Fascism, Fiction*, London: Penguin.

Royal Academy (1963) *Illustrated Summer Exhibition Catalogue*, London: Royal Academy of Arts.

Rubenstein, M. (2007) 'Why the DRC's legal strategy succeeded', in Disability Rights Commission (2007) 'DRC legal achievements 2000–2007', London: DRC, pp 11–14.

Salem, K. and Doyle, M. (2023) 'Promoting mediation to resolve administrative disputes in Council of Europe member states (part 2): administrative mediation in the UK', REALaw blog, Available from: https://wp.me/pcQ0x2-CL

Sandel, M. (2005) *Public Philosophy: Essays on Morality in Politics*, Cambridge, MA: Harvard University Press.

Sandford, J. (1976) *Cathy Come Home*, London: Marion BOYARS Publishers.

Sayce, L. (2000) *From Psychiatric Patient to Citizen: Overcoming Discrimination and Social Exclusion*, Basingstoke: Macmillan.

Sayce, L. (2016) *From Psychiatric Patient to Citizen Revisited*, London: Palgrave.

Schiavone, A. (2012) *The Invention of Law in the West*, trans J. Carden and A. Shugaar, Cambridge, MA: Harvard University Press.

Scott, J. (1998) *Seeing Like a State: How Certain Schemes to Improve the Human Condition Have Failed*, New Haven: Yale University Press.

Scruton, R. (2002) *The West and the Rest: Globalization and the Terrorist Threat*, London: Bloomsbury.

Secretary of State for Education (2019) 'Timpson review of school exclusion', CP 92, London: The Stationery Office.

Secretary of State for Education (2022) 'SEND review: right support, right place, right time', CP 624, London: HM Stationery Office.

Secretary of State for Health and Social Care and the Lord Chancellor and Secretary of State for Justice (2021) 'Reforming the Mental Health Act', CP 355, London: HM Stationery Office.

Seddon, J. (2008) *Systems Thinking in the Public Sector*, Axminster: Triarchy Press.

Shklar, J. (1966) 'In defense of legalism', *Journal of Legal Education*, 19(1): 51–8.

Shklar, J. (1986) *Legalism: Law, Morals and Political Trials*, Cambridge, MA: Harvard University Press.

Shklar, J. (1987) 'Political theory and the rule of law', in A. Hutchinson and P. Monaghan (eds) *The Rule of Law: Ideal or Ideology*, Toronto: Carswell, pp 1–16.

Shonfield, A. (1965) *Modern Capitalism: The Changing Balance of Public and Private Power*, London: Oxford University Press.

Simon, W. (2004) 'Solving problems v claiming rights: the pragmatist challenge to legal liberalism', *William and Mary Law Review*, 46(1): 127–212.

Skinner, Q. (1986) 'The artist as political philosopher', *Proceedings of the British Academy*, 72: 1–56.

Skinner, Q. (2003–4) 'Picturing perfect government', *Wissenschaftskolleg zu Berlin, Jahrbuch*, 318: 306–24.

Smith, G. and Hughes, T. (2021) *Democracy in a Pandemic: Participation in Response to Crisis*, London: University of Westminster Press.

Somek, A. (2014) *The Cosmopolitan Constitution*, Oxford: Oxford University Press.

Spandler, H., Anderson, J. and Sapey, B. (2015) *Madness, Distress and the Politics of Disablement*, Bristol: Policy Press.

Stacey, F. (1971) *The British Ombudsman*, Oxford: Clarendon Press.

Stapelton, J. (1994) *Englishness and the Study of Politics: The Social and Political Thought of Ernest Barker*, Cambridge: Cambridge University Press.

Stapleton, J. (2014) 'T.E. Utley and the renewal of conservatism in post-war Britain', *Journal of Political Ideologies*, 19(2): 207–26.

Stears, M. (2021) *Out of the Ordinary: How Everyday Life Inspired a Nation and How It Can Again*, Cambridge, MA: Harvard University Press.

Stuhmcke, A. 'Government watchdog agencies and administrative justice', in M. Hertogh, R. Kirkham, R. Thomas and J. Tomlinson (eds) *The Oxford Handbook of Administrative Justice*, Oxford: Oxford University Press, pp 115–36.

Taylor, C. (2004) *Modern Social Imaginaries*, Durham: Duke University Press.

Taylor, C., Nanz, P. and Taylor, M. (2020) *Reconstructing Democracy: How Citizens Are Building from the Ground Up*, Cambridge, MA: Harvard University Press.

Terzi, L. (ed) (2010) *Special Educational Needs: A New Look*, London: Bloomsbury.

Thomas, R. (2022) *Administrative Law in Action: Immigration Administration*, Oxford: Hart.

Titmuss, R. (1971) 'Welfare "rights", law and discretion', *Political Quarterly*, 42(2): 113–32.

Tomkins, A. (2005) *Our Republican Constitution*, Oxford: Hart.

Toynbee, P. and Walker, D. (2017) *Dismembered: How the Attack on the State Harms Us All*, London: Guardian Books.

United Nations, Office of the High Commissioner for Human Rights (2007) *Disabilities: Handbook for Parliamentarians*, Geneva: United Nations.

United Nations (2020) 'Resolution on ombudsman and mediator institutions', Geneva: United Nations.

Utley, T. (1961) *Occasion for Ombudsman*, London: Christopher Johnson.

Vanhala, L. (2011) *Making Rights a Reality? Disability Rights Activists and Legal Mobilization*, Cambridge: Cambridge University Press.

Vanhala, L. (2015) 'The diffusion of disability rights in Europe', *Human Rights Quarterly*, 37(4): 831–53.

Veasey, M. (2019) 'An insistence on freedom: Siegfried Charoux's Civilization Cycles', *Sculpture Journal*, 28(1): 123–38.

Venice Commission (2011) 'Rule of law checklist', Strasbourg: Council of Europe.

Venice Commission (2019) 'Principles on the protection and promotion of the ombudsman institution', Strasbourg: Council of Europe.

Vermeule, A. (2020) 'Beyond originalism', *The Atlantic*, 31 March.

Vermeule, A. (2022) *Common Good Constitutionalism*, Cambridge: Polity.

Warnock, M. (1978) 'Report of the Committee of Enquiry into the Education of Handicapped Children and Young People', London: HMSO.

Warnock, M. (2003) *Nature and Morality: Recollections of a Philosopher in Public Life*, London: Continuum.

Warnock, M. (2010) 'Special educational needs: a new look', in L. Terzi (ed) *Special Educational Needs: A New Look*, London: Bloomsbury, pp 11–45.

Weller, P. (2010) 'Lost in translation: human rights and mental health law', in B. McSherry and P. Weller (eds) *Rethinking Rights-Based Mental Health Laws*, Oxford: Hart, pp 51–72.

Weller, P. (2011) 'Taking a reflexive turn: non-adversarial justice and mental health review tribunals', *Monash University Law Review*, 37(1): 81–101.

Wexler, D. and Winick, B. (1991) *Essays in Therapeutic Jurisprudence*, Durham, NC: Carolina Academic Press.

Whyatt, Sir J. (1961) *The Citizen and the Administration: The Redress of Grievances*, London: Stevens & Sons.

Wiener, M. (1971) *Between Two Worlds: The Political Thought of Graham Wallas*, Oxford: Clarendon Press.

Williams, J., Gill, C. and Hirst, C. (2022) 'Towards therapeutic complaints resolution', in M. Groves and A. Stuhmcke (eds) *The Ombudsman in the Modern State*, Oxford: Hart, pp 265–86.

Williams, R. (1958) 'Culture is ordinary', in Mackenzie, N. (ed) *Conviction*, London: MacGibbon and Kee, pp 74–92.

Williams, W. (2020) 'Windrush lessons learned review', HC 93, London: HM Stationery Office.

Wilson, H. (1964) *Labour Party News Release*, 3 July, 1964.

Woolf, The Rt Hon Lord (1996) 'Access to justice: final report', London: Stationery Office.

World Health Organization (2003) 'The mental health context', Geneva: WHO.

Wright, T. (2012) *Doing Politics*, London: Biteback.

Zacka, B. (2017) *When the State Meets the Street: Public Service and Moral Agency*, Cambridge, MA: Harvard University Press.

Zimmern, A. (1911) *The Greek Commonwealth*, Oxford: Clarendon Press.

Zimmern, A. (1930) 'Democracy and the expert', *Political Quarterly*, 1(1): 7–25.

Zimmern, A. (1936) *The League of Nations and the Rule of Law 1918–1935*, London: Macmillan and Co.

Index

www.ingramcontent.com/pod-product-compliance
Lightning Source LLC
Chambersburg PA
CBHW071417210326
41597CB00020B/3546